Real speedo blokes

Sketeched

R GINRO

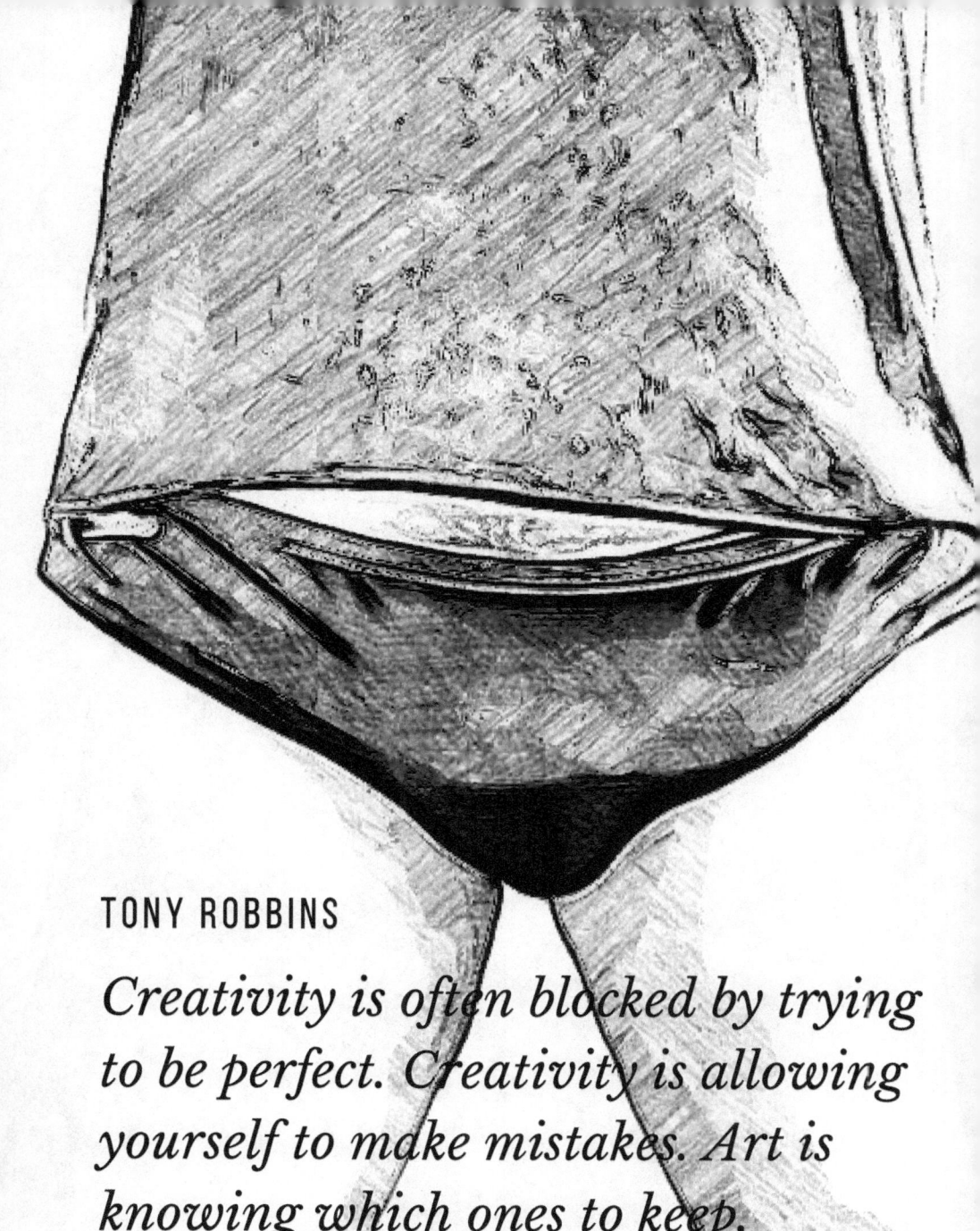

TONY ROBBINS

Creativity is often blocked by trying to be perfect. Creativity is allowing yourself to make mistakes. Art is knowing which ones to keep.

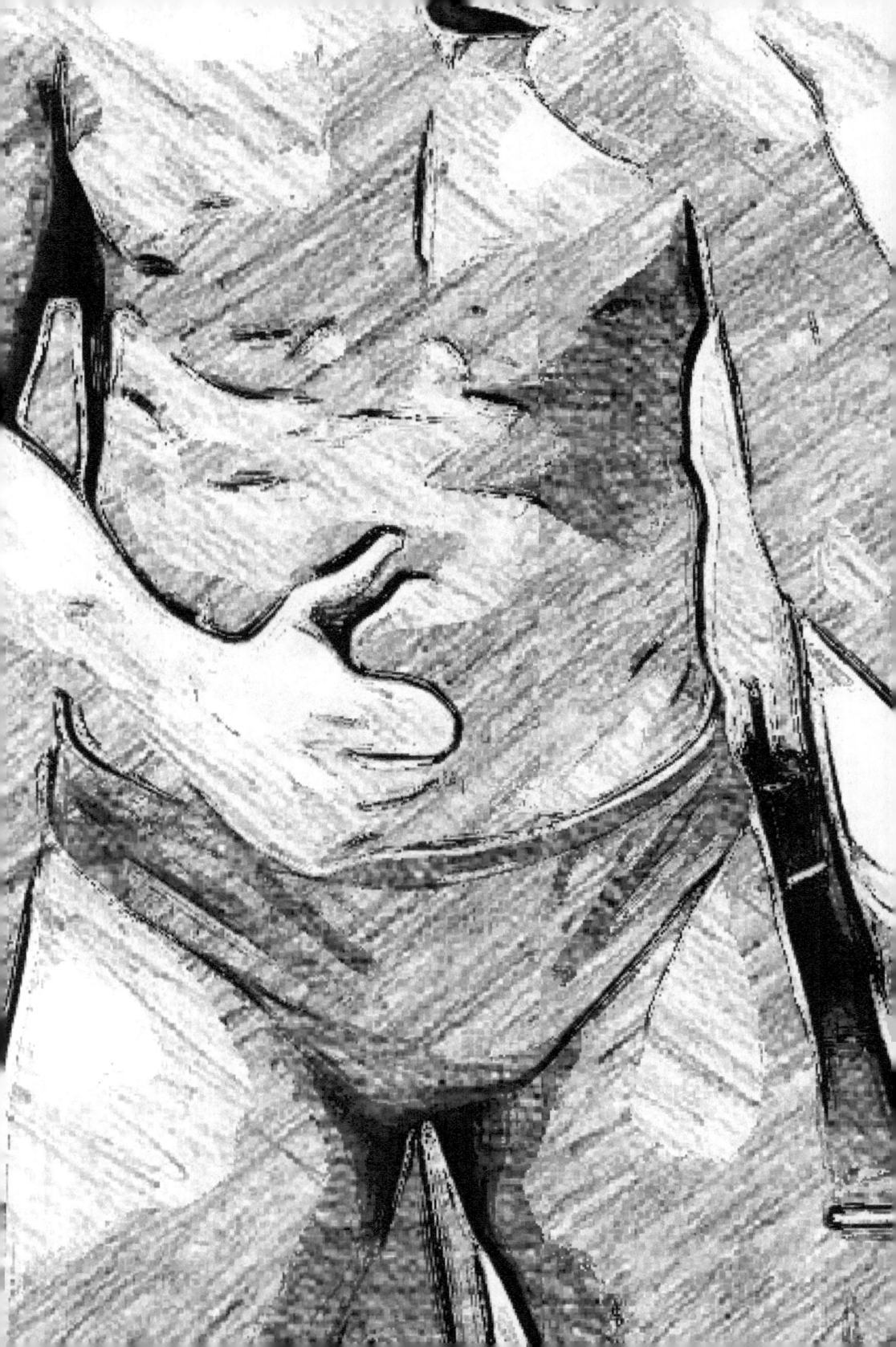

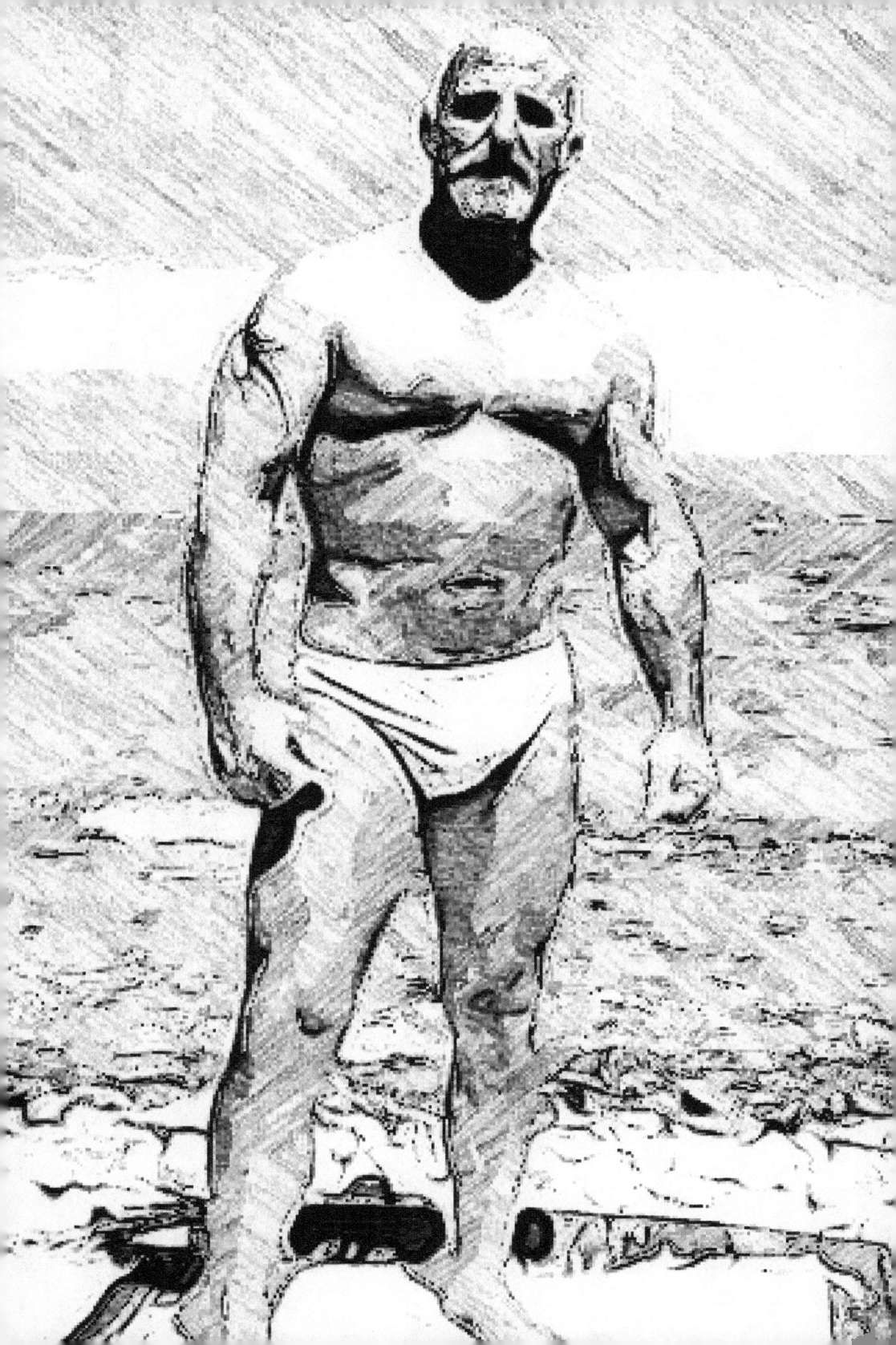

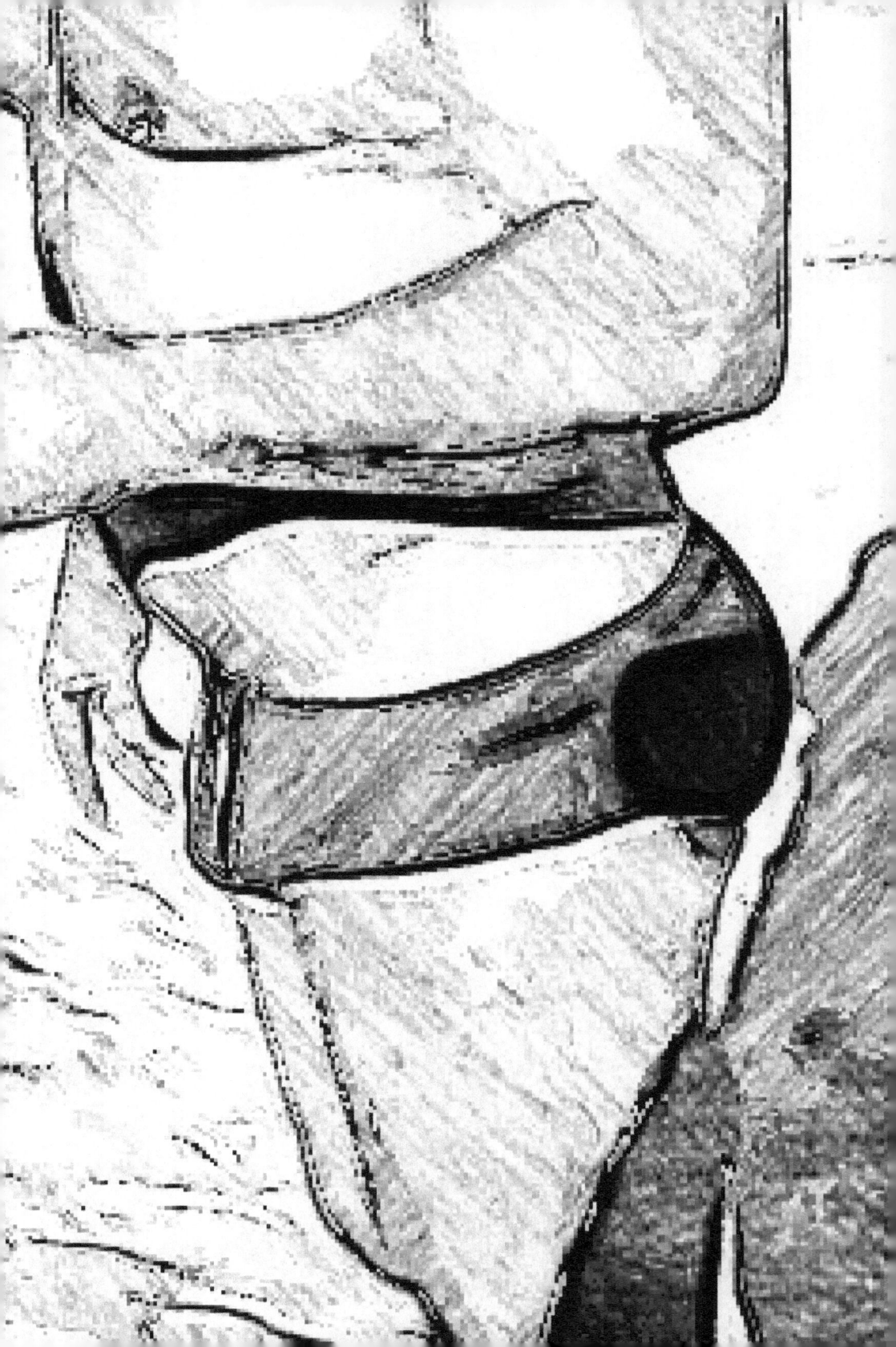

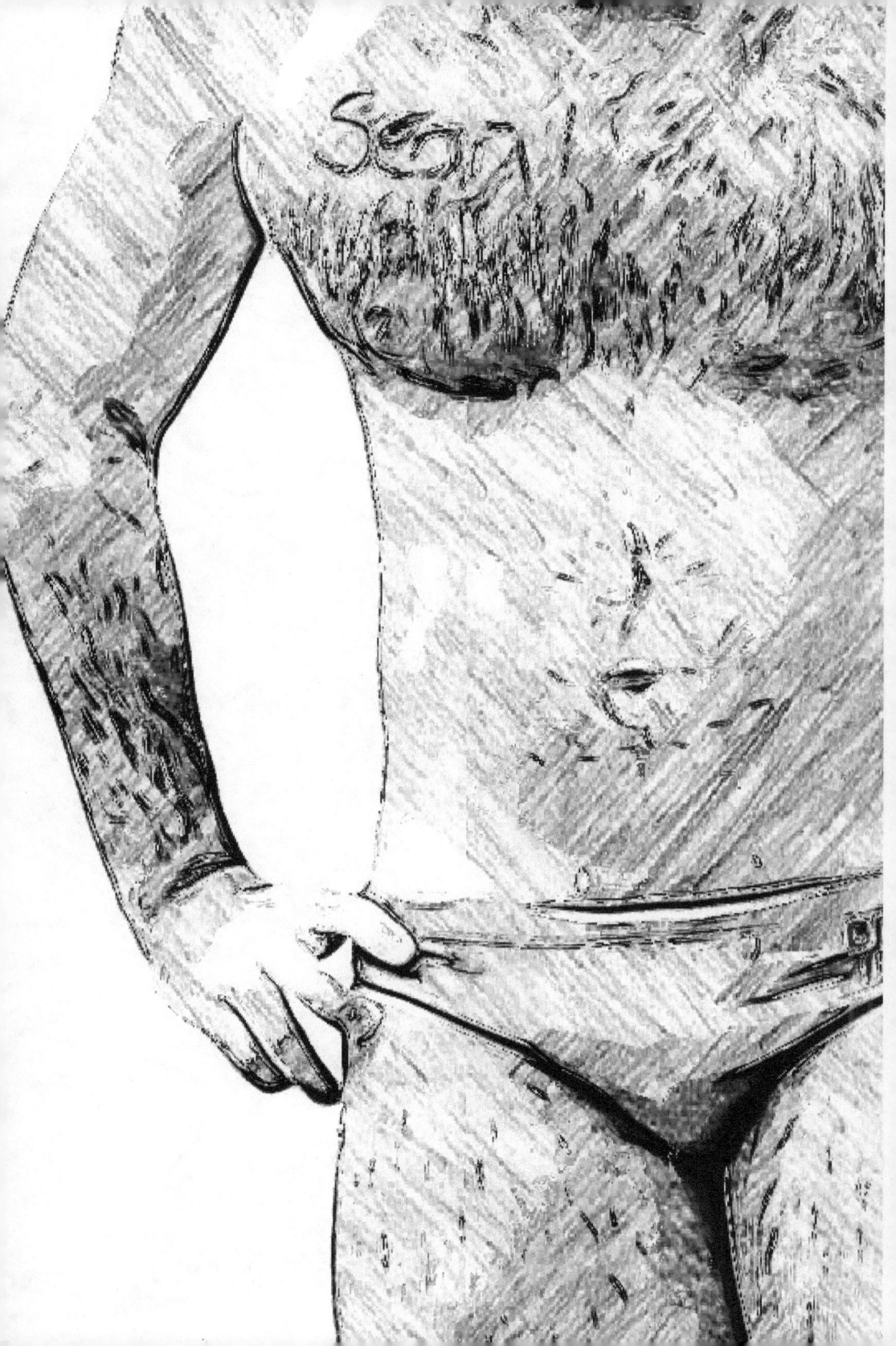

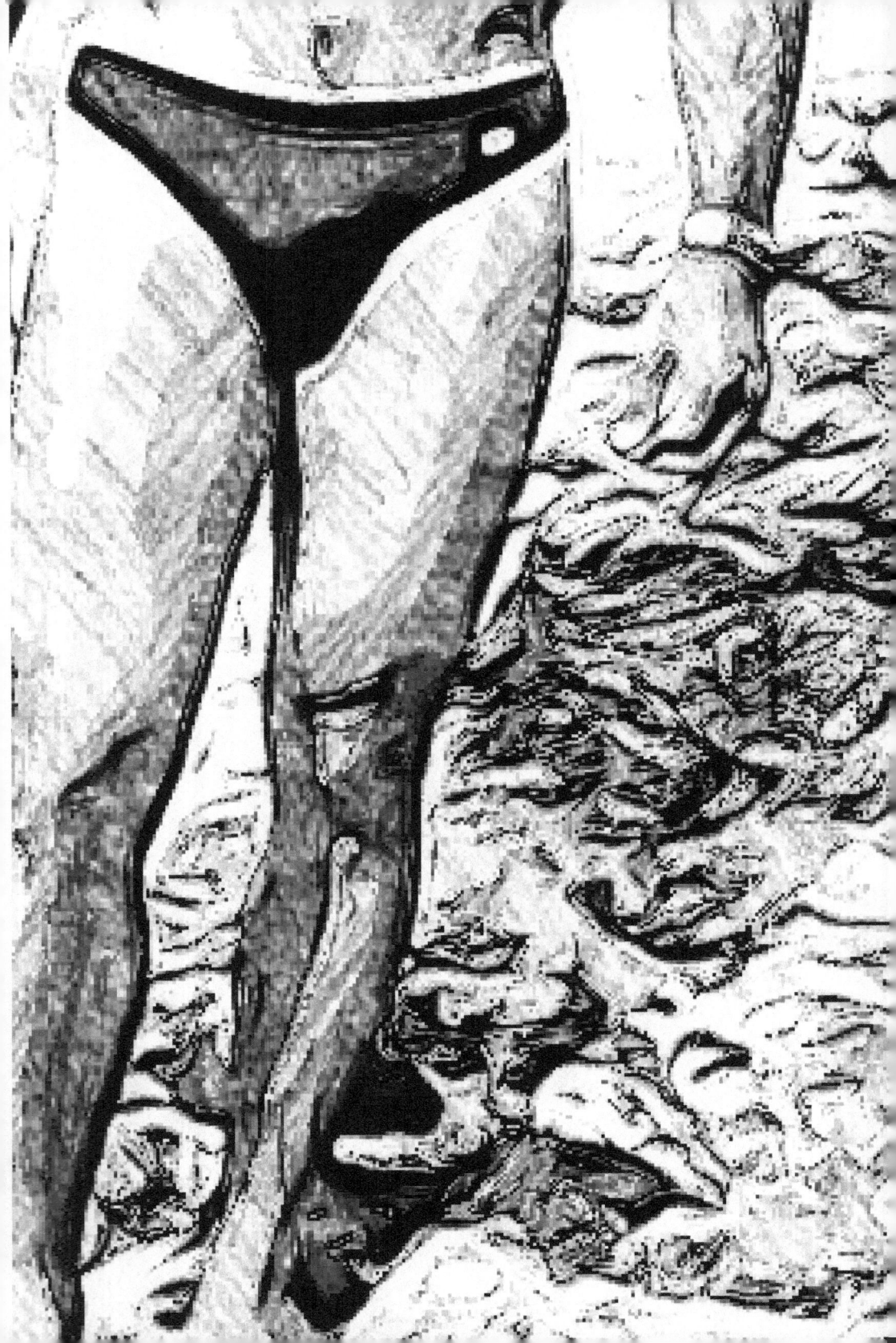

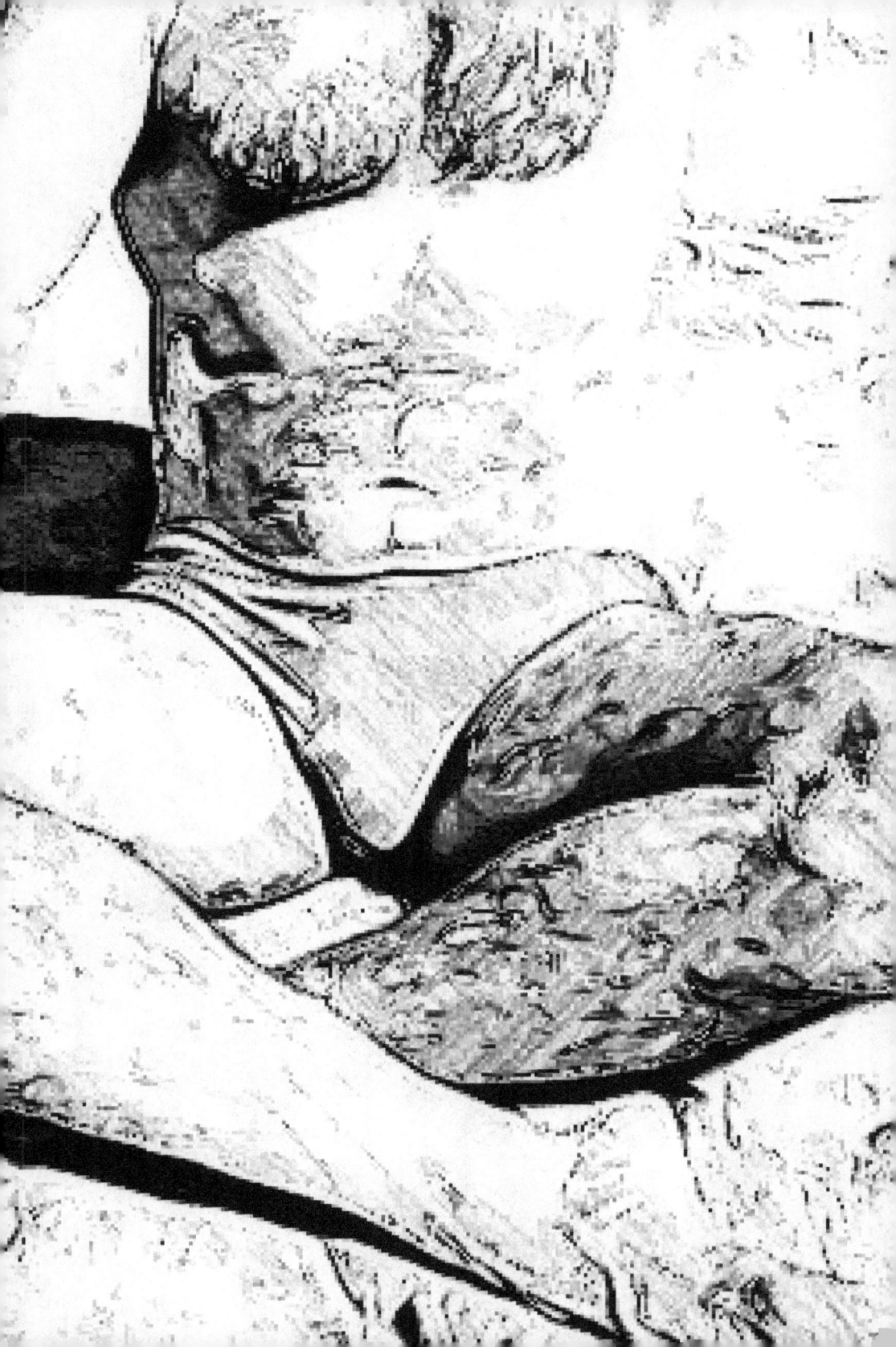

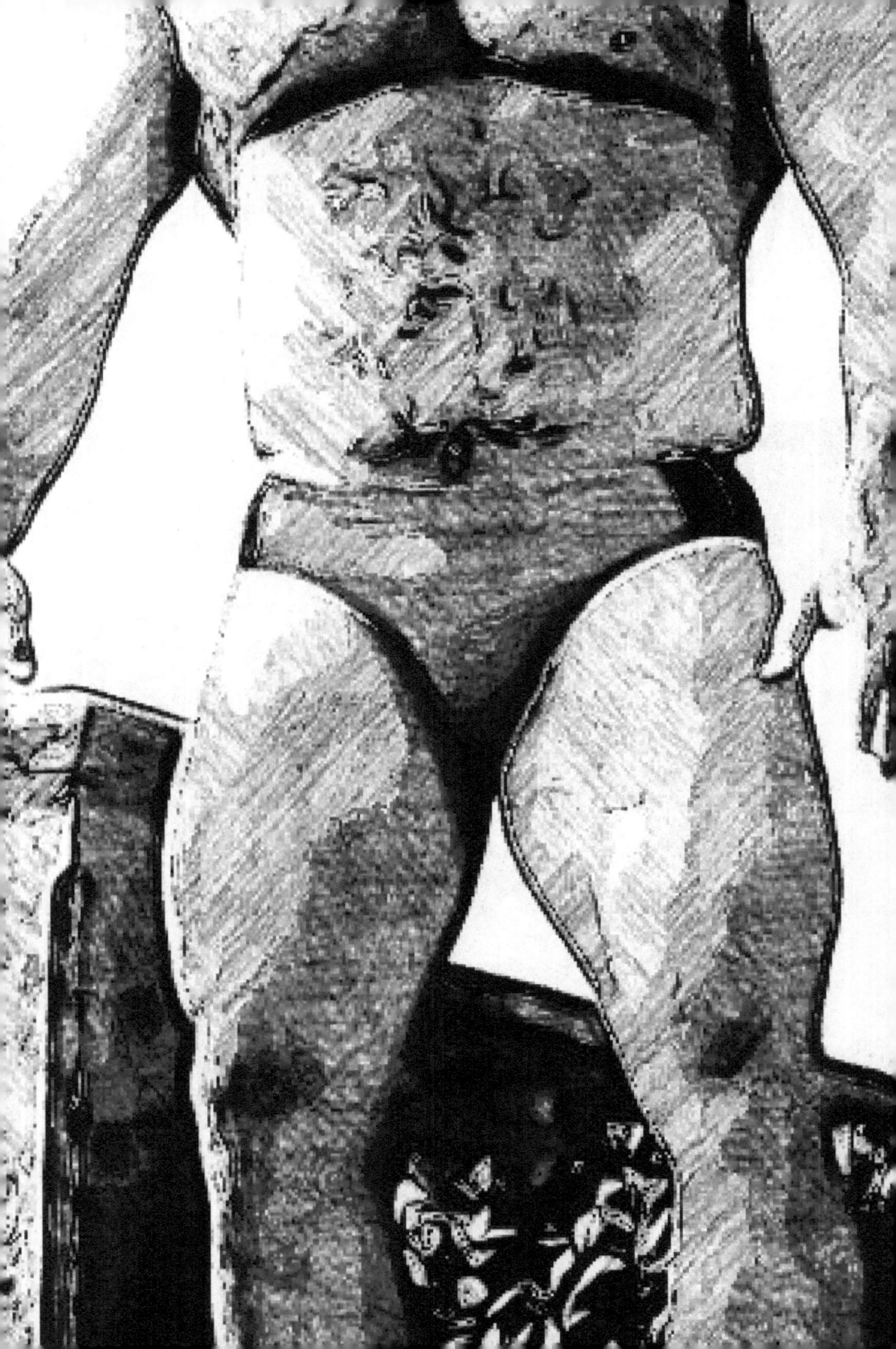

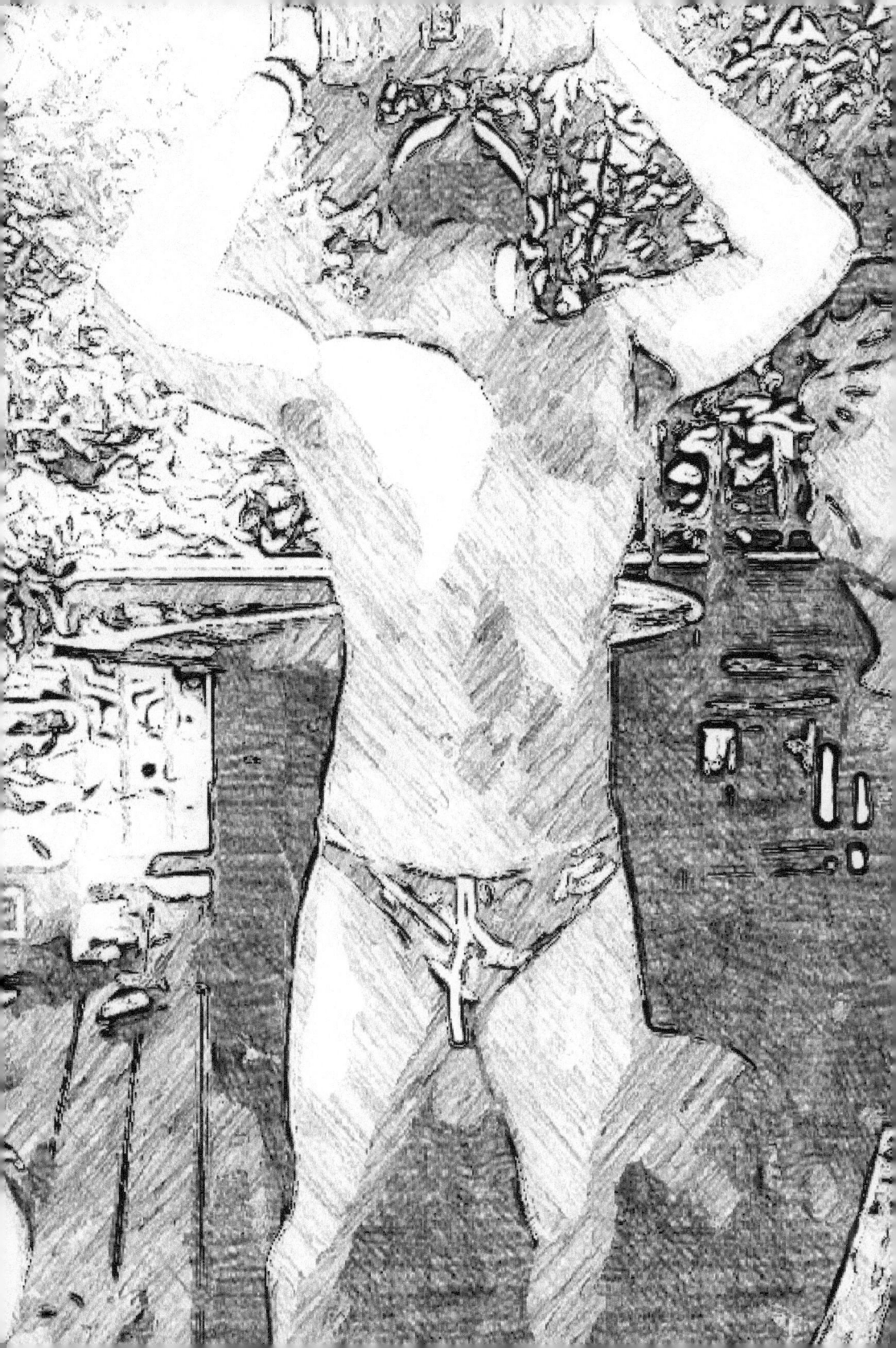

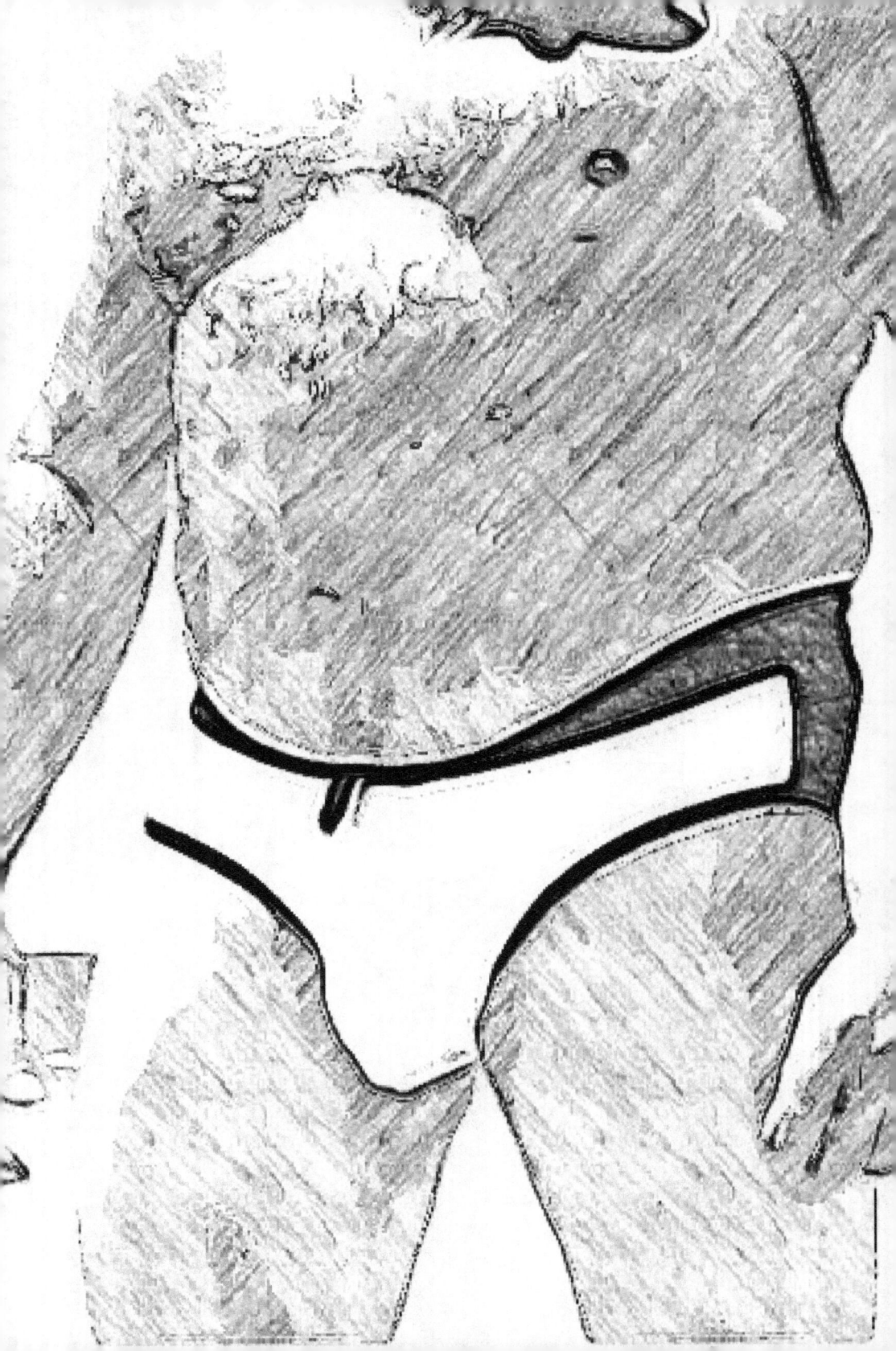

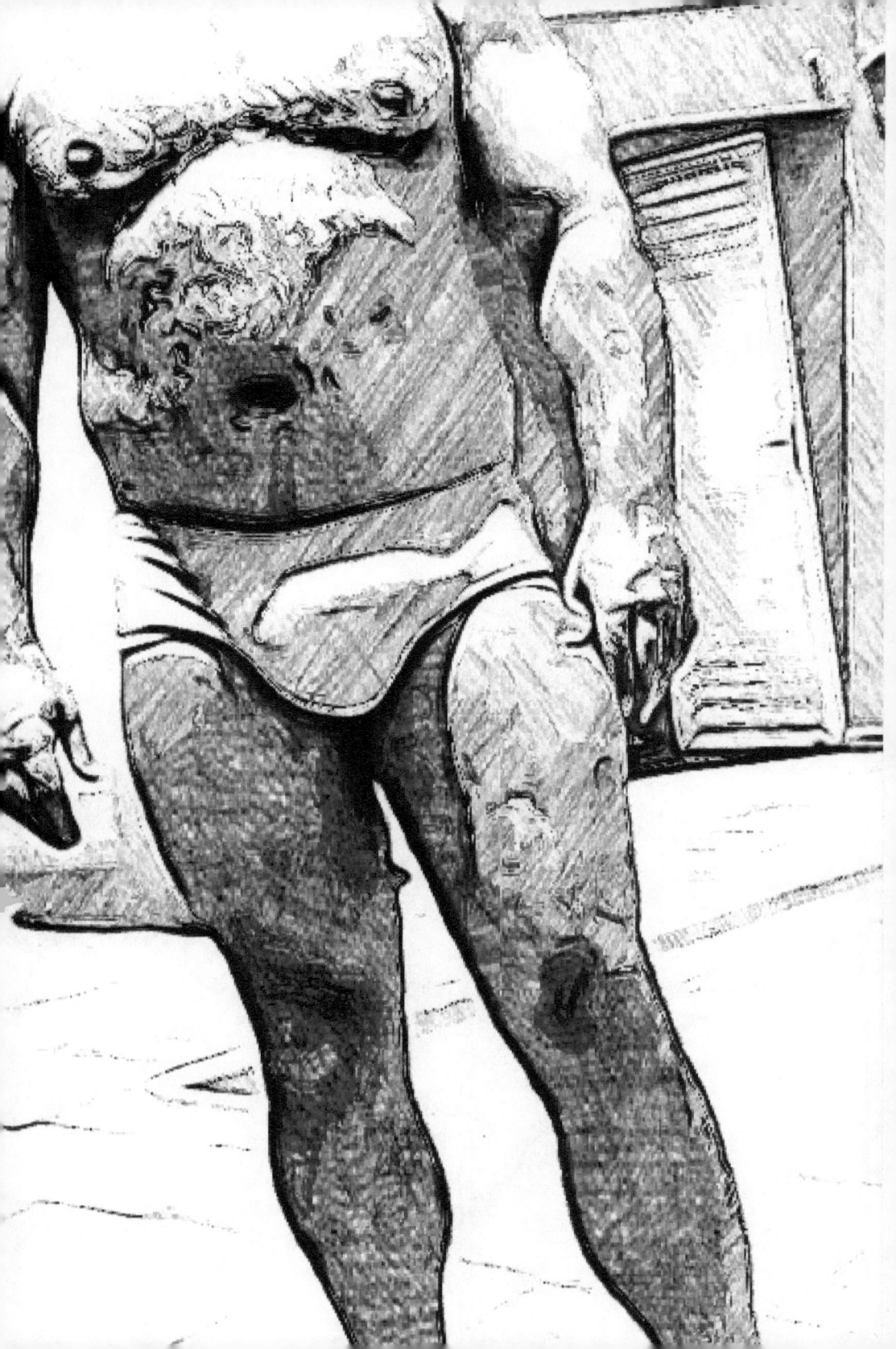

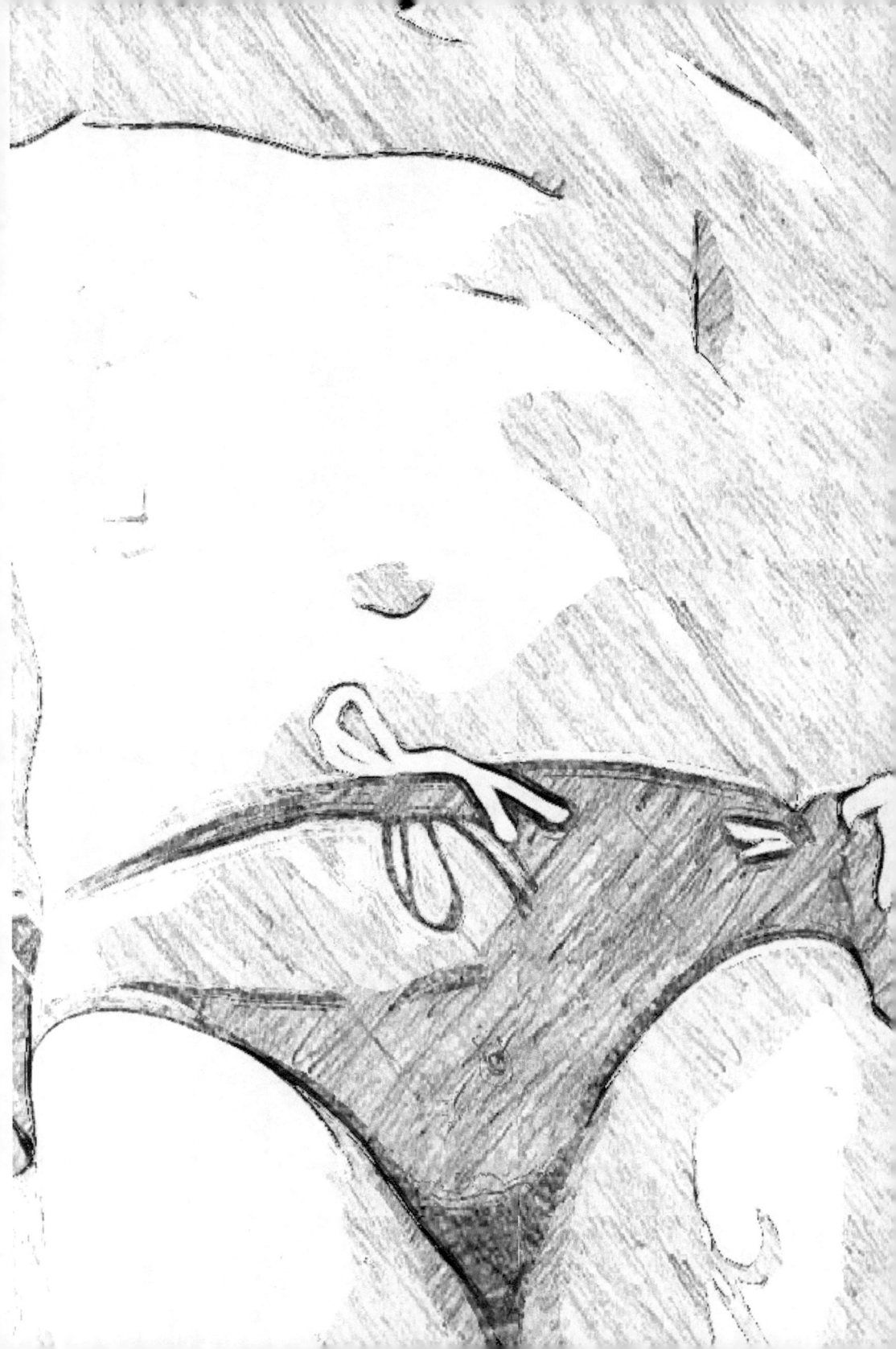

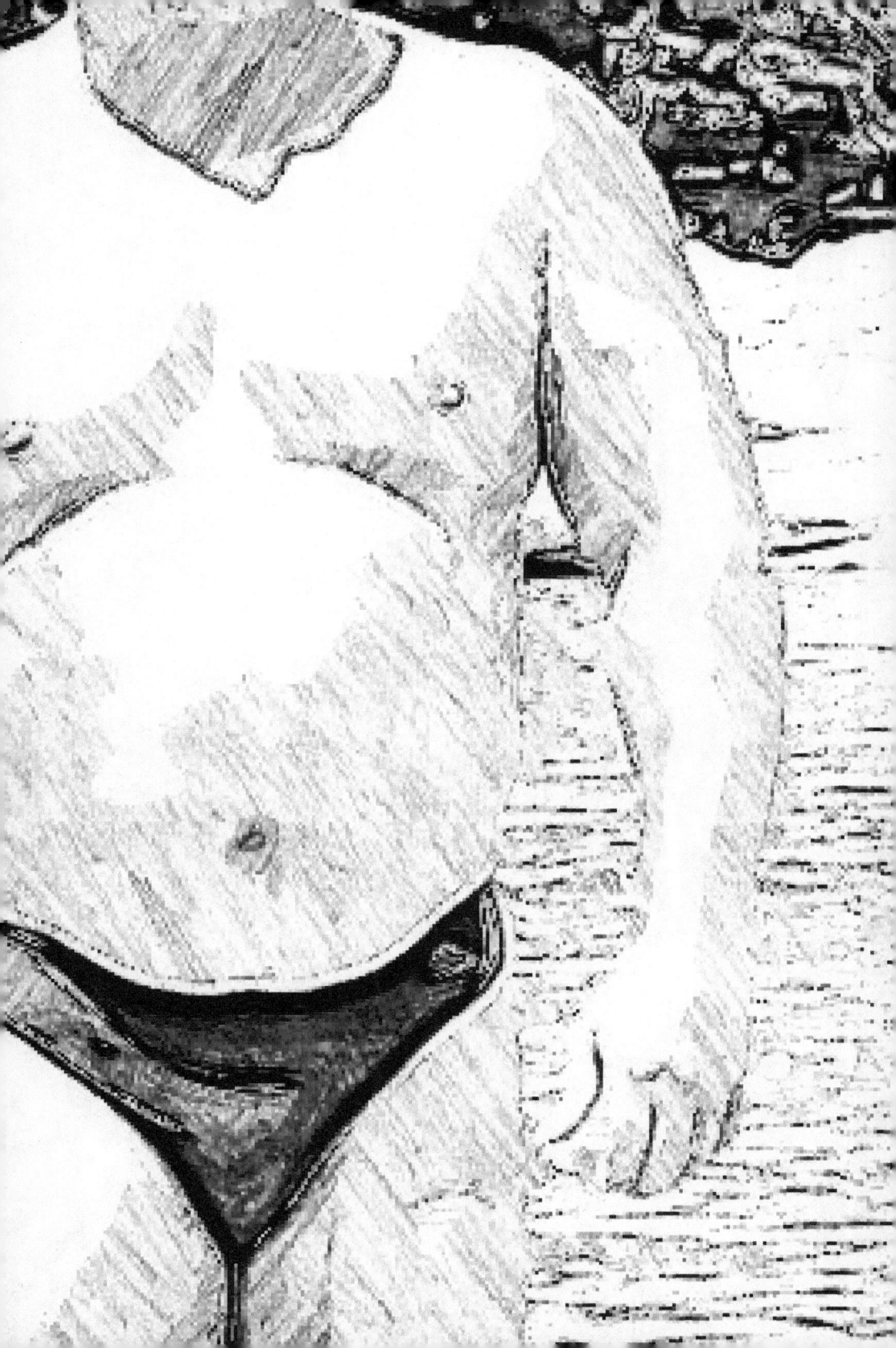

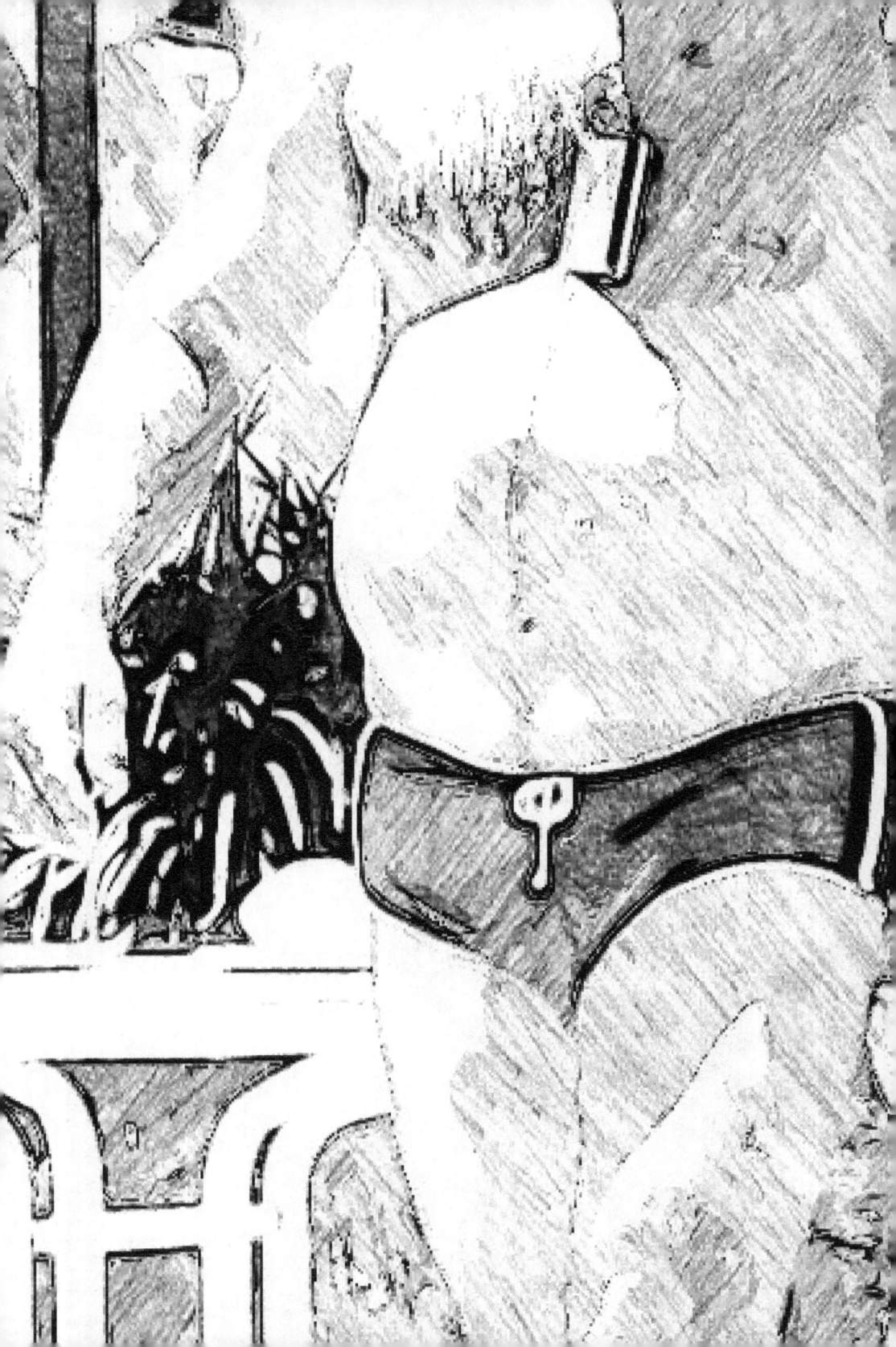

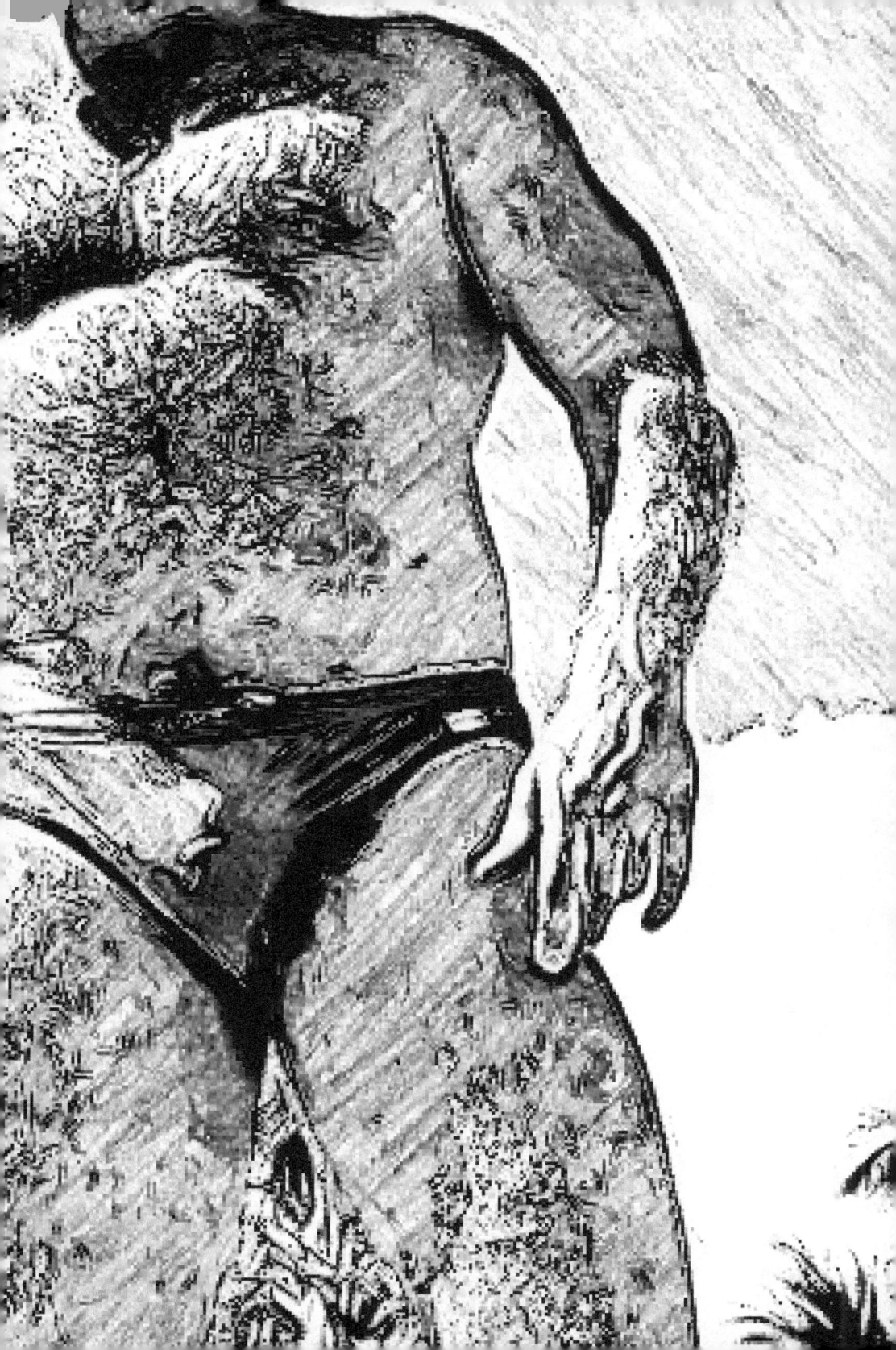

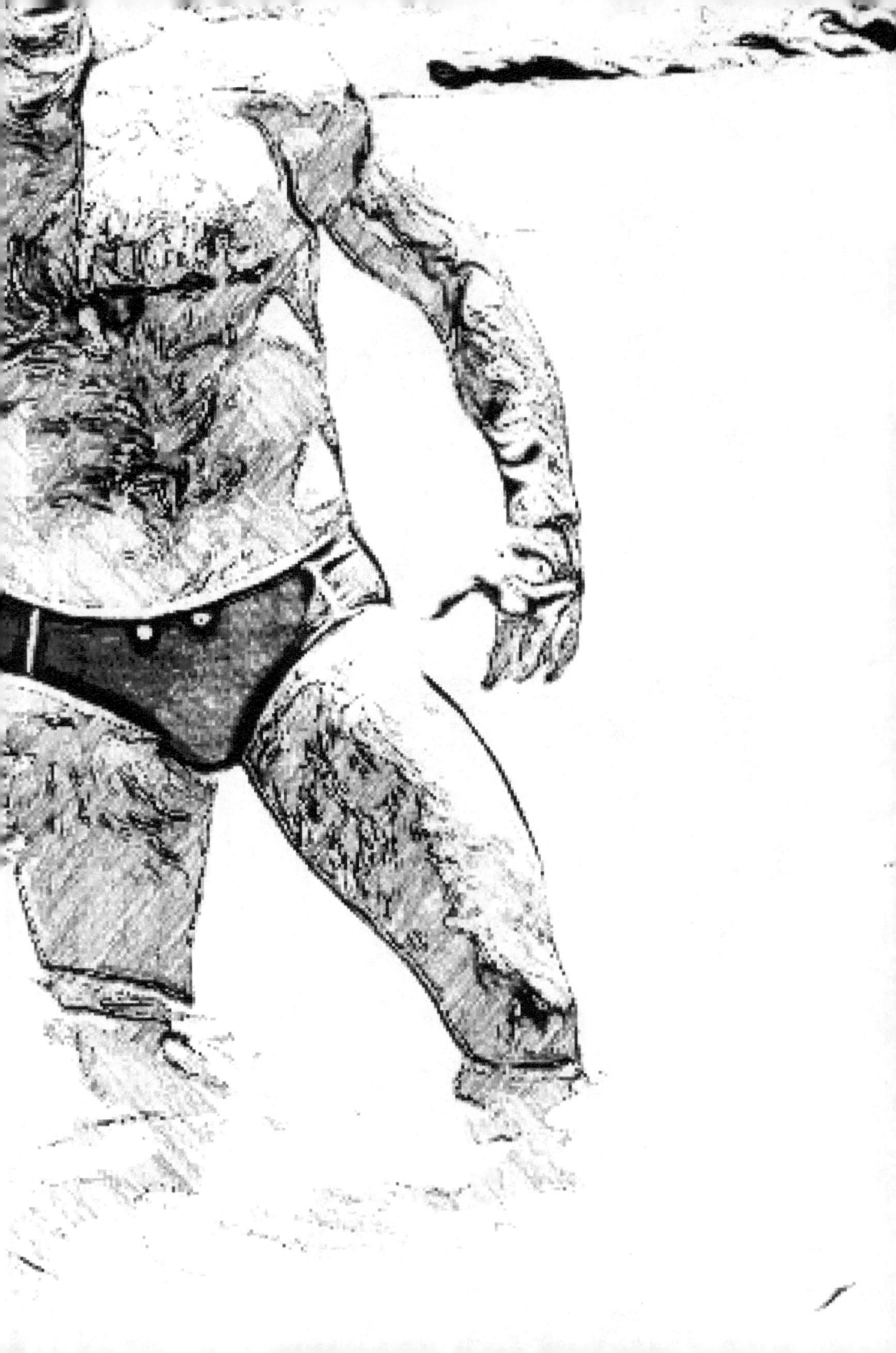

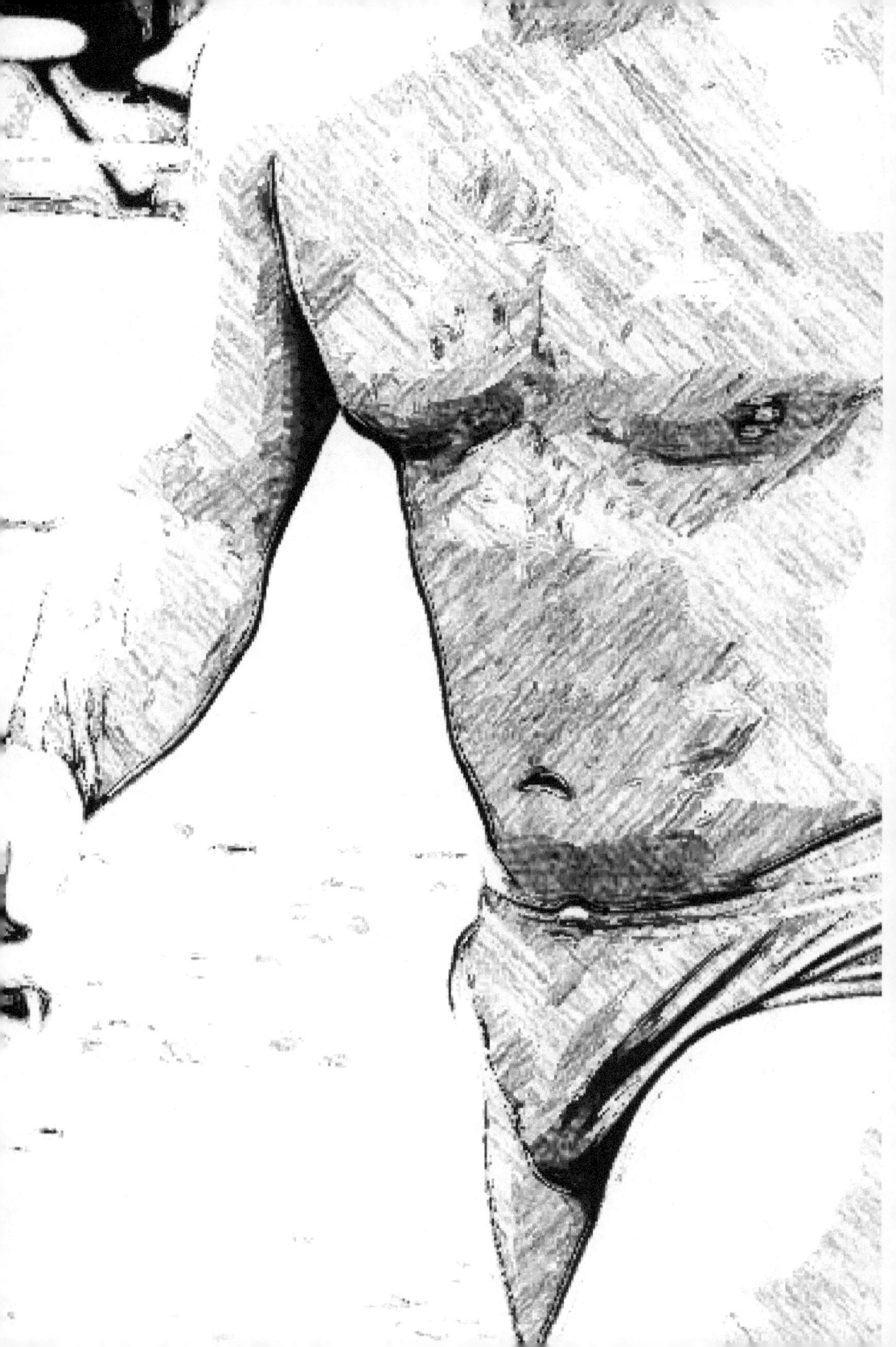

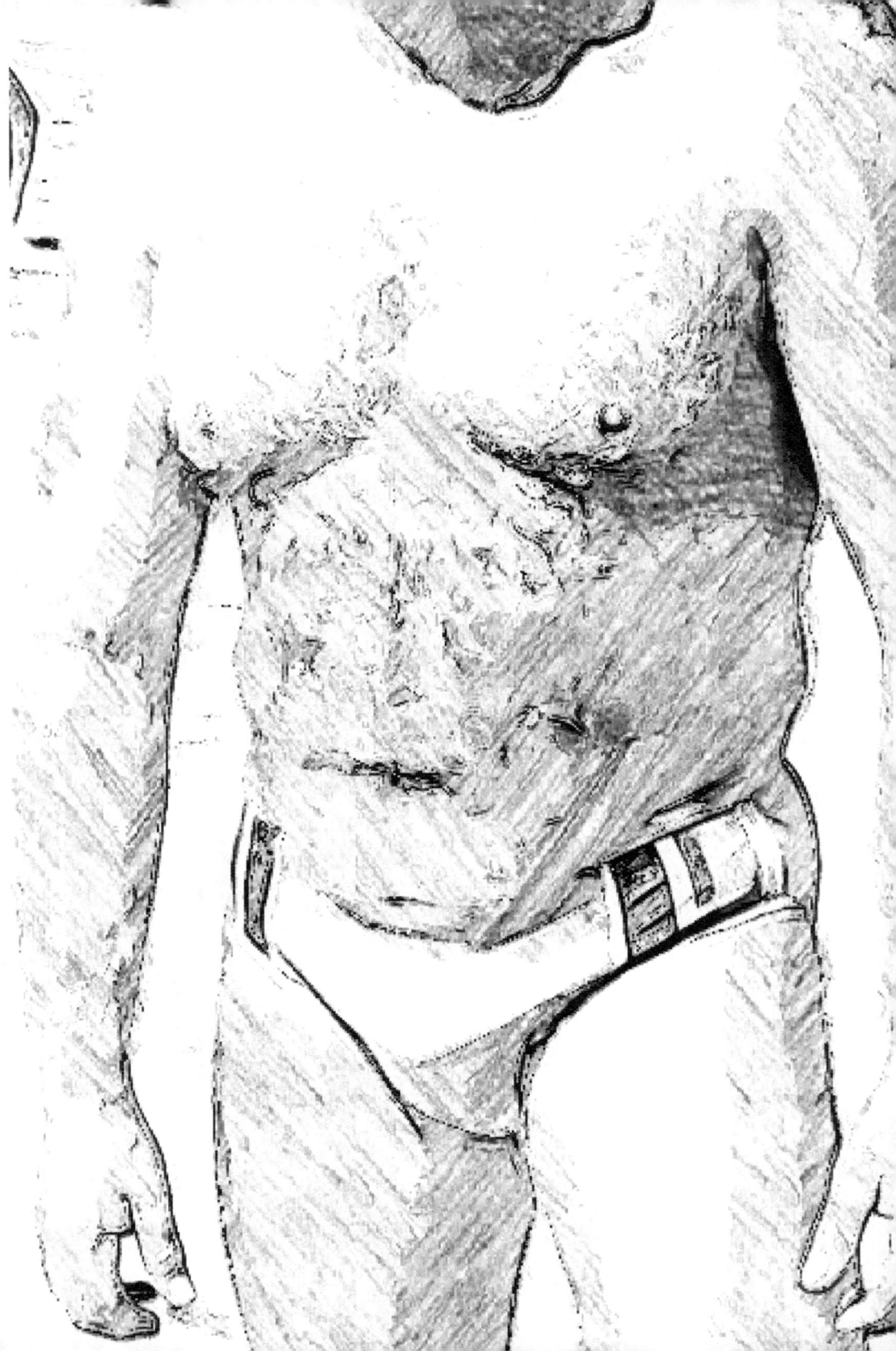

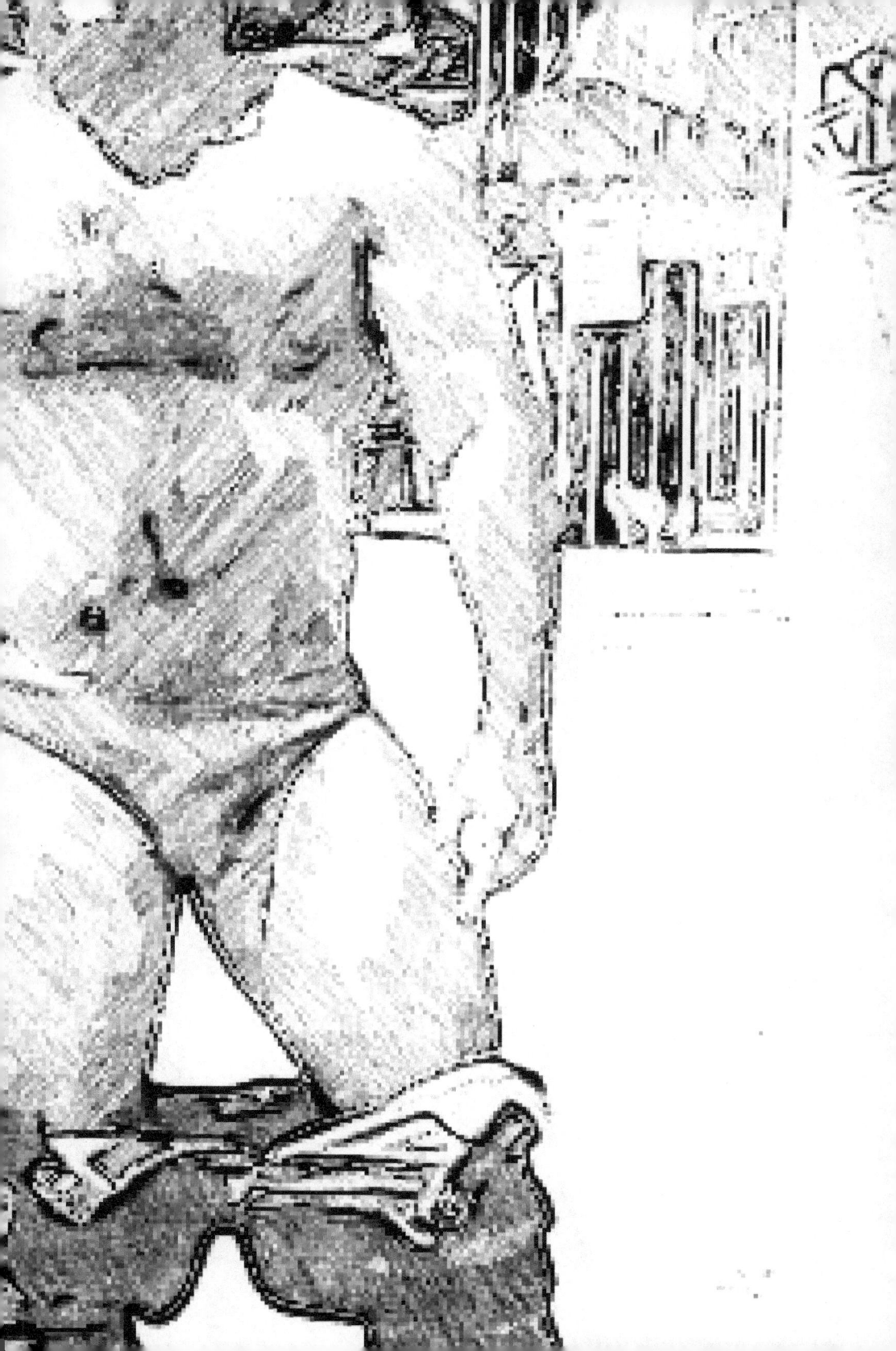

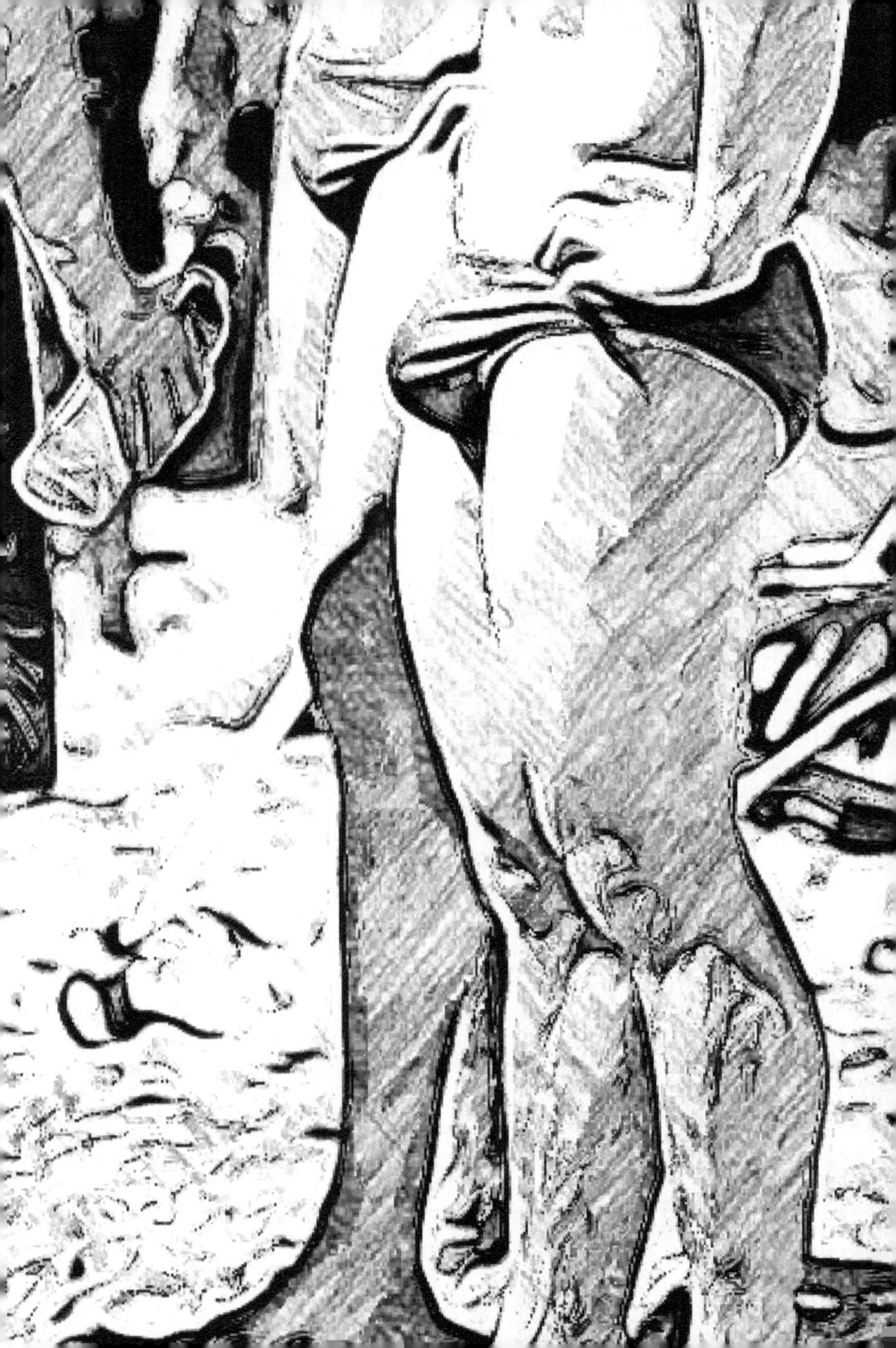

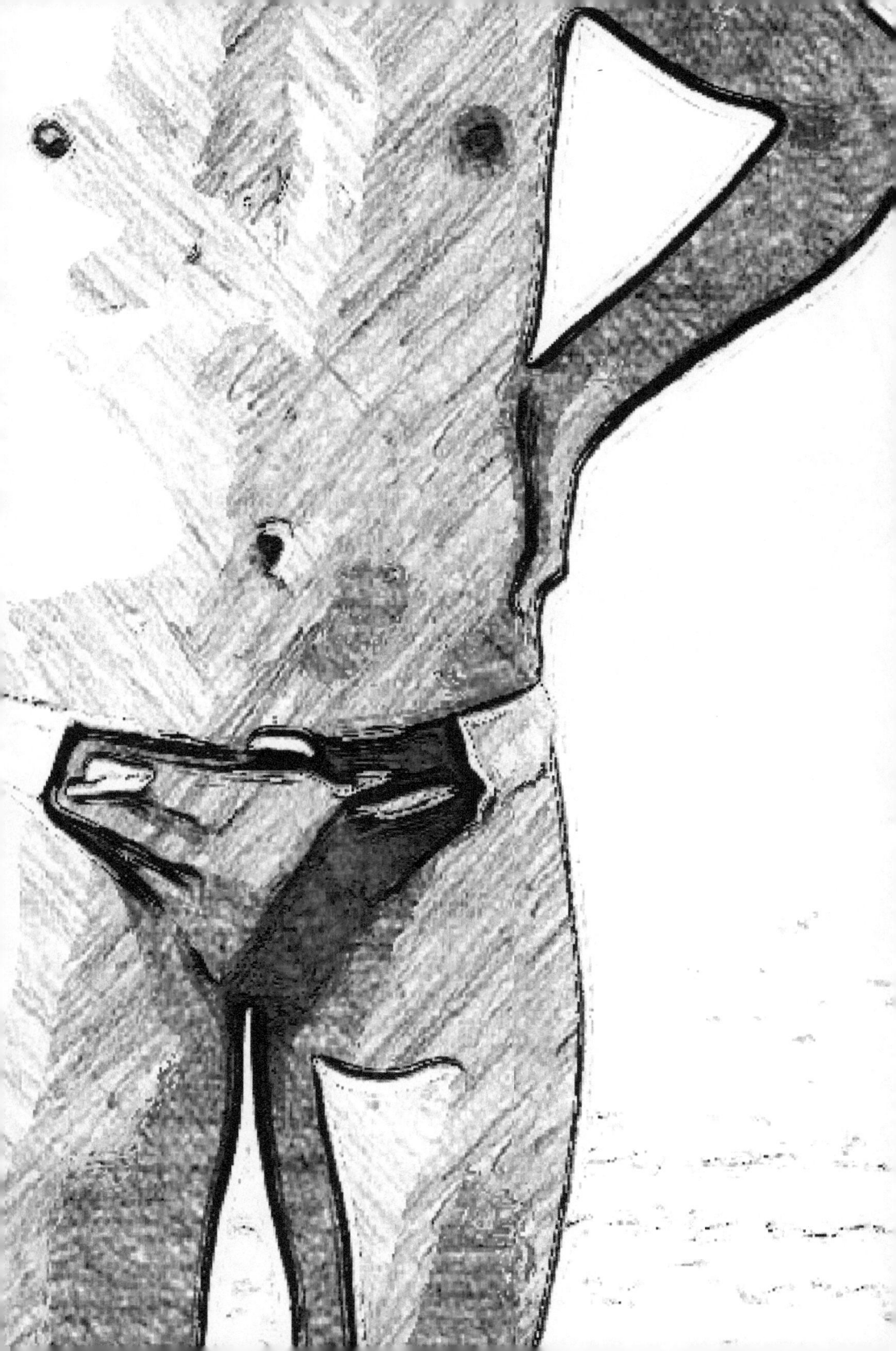

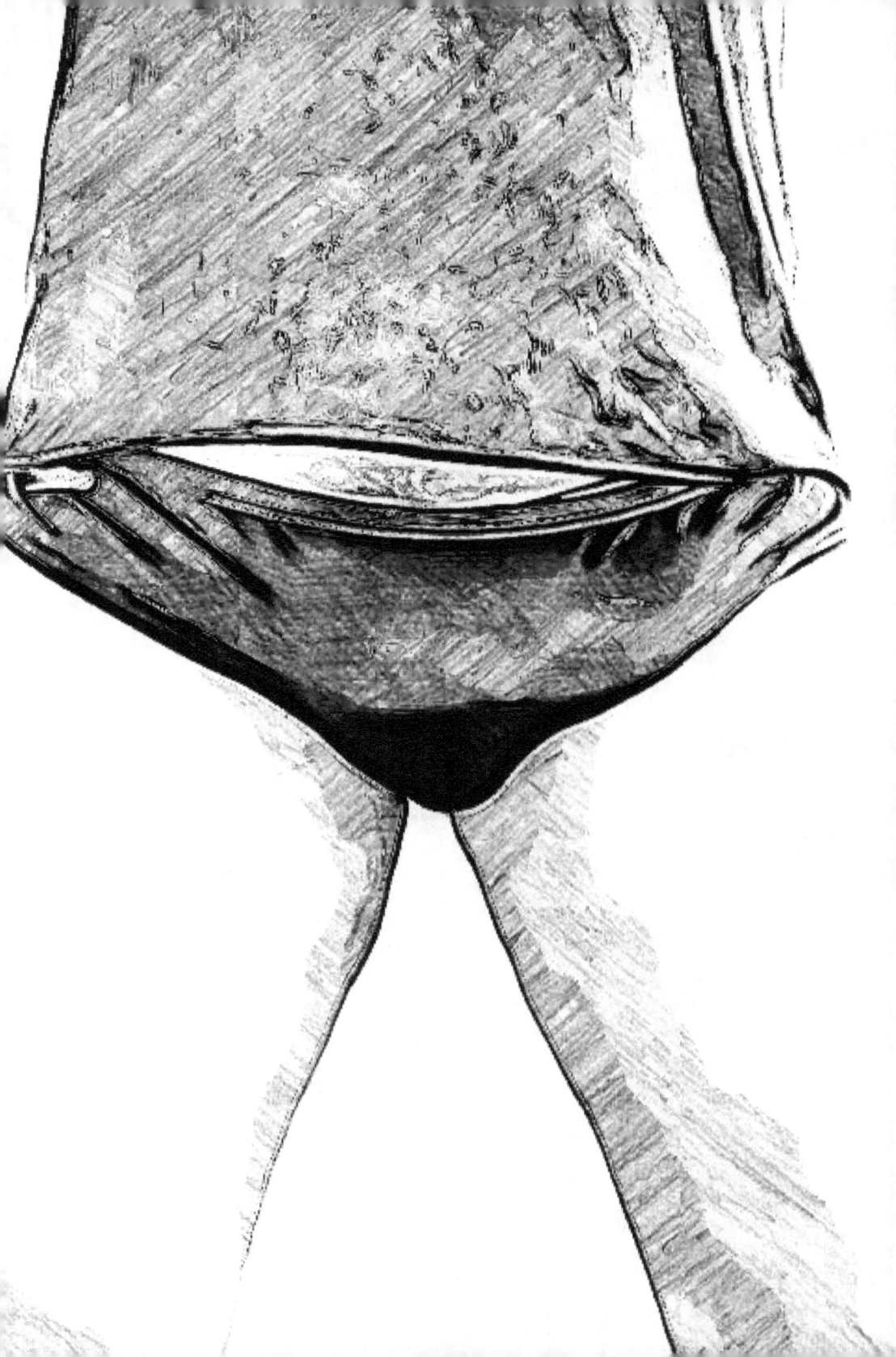

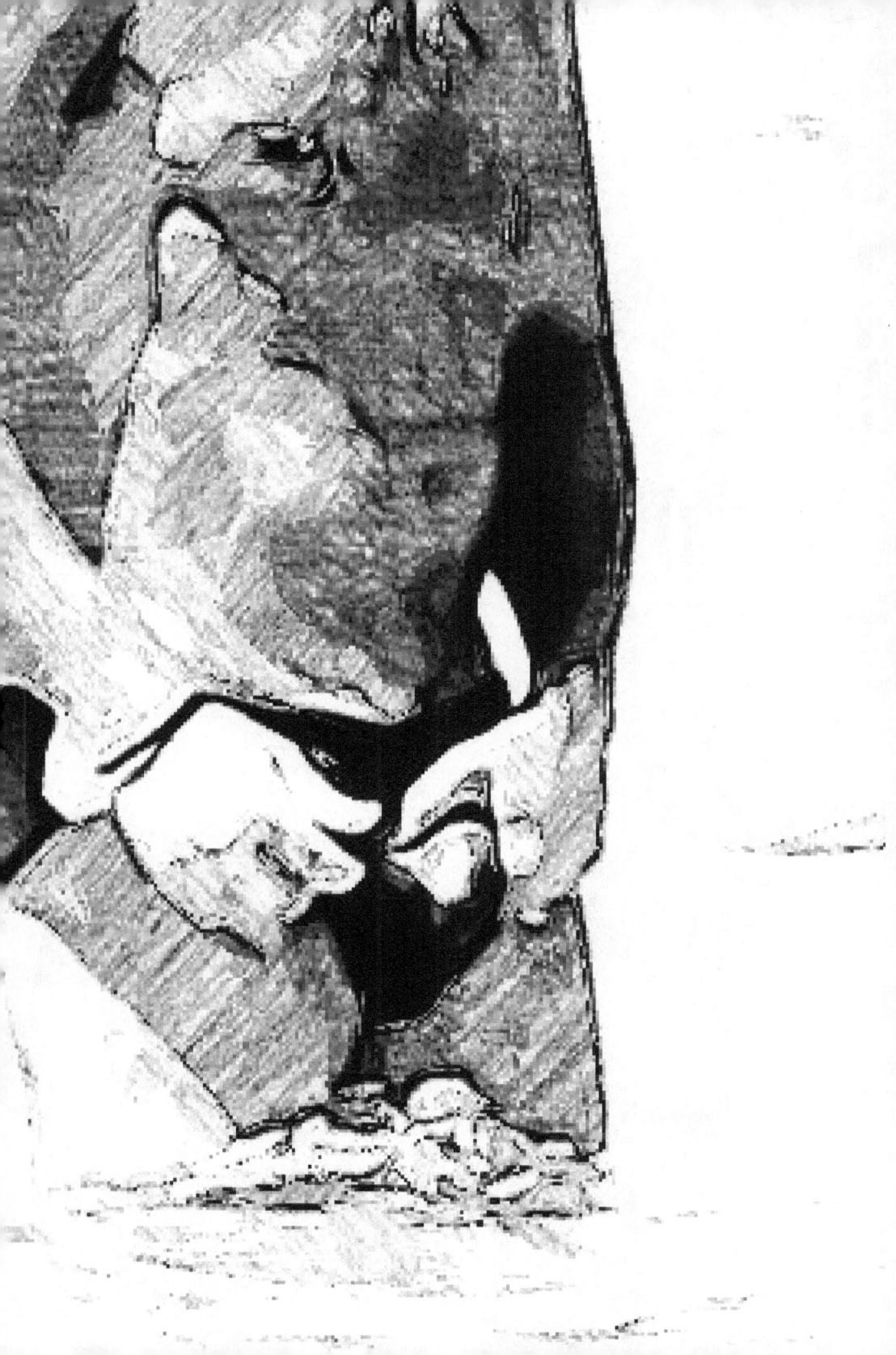

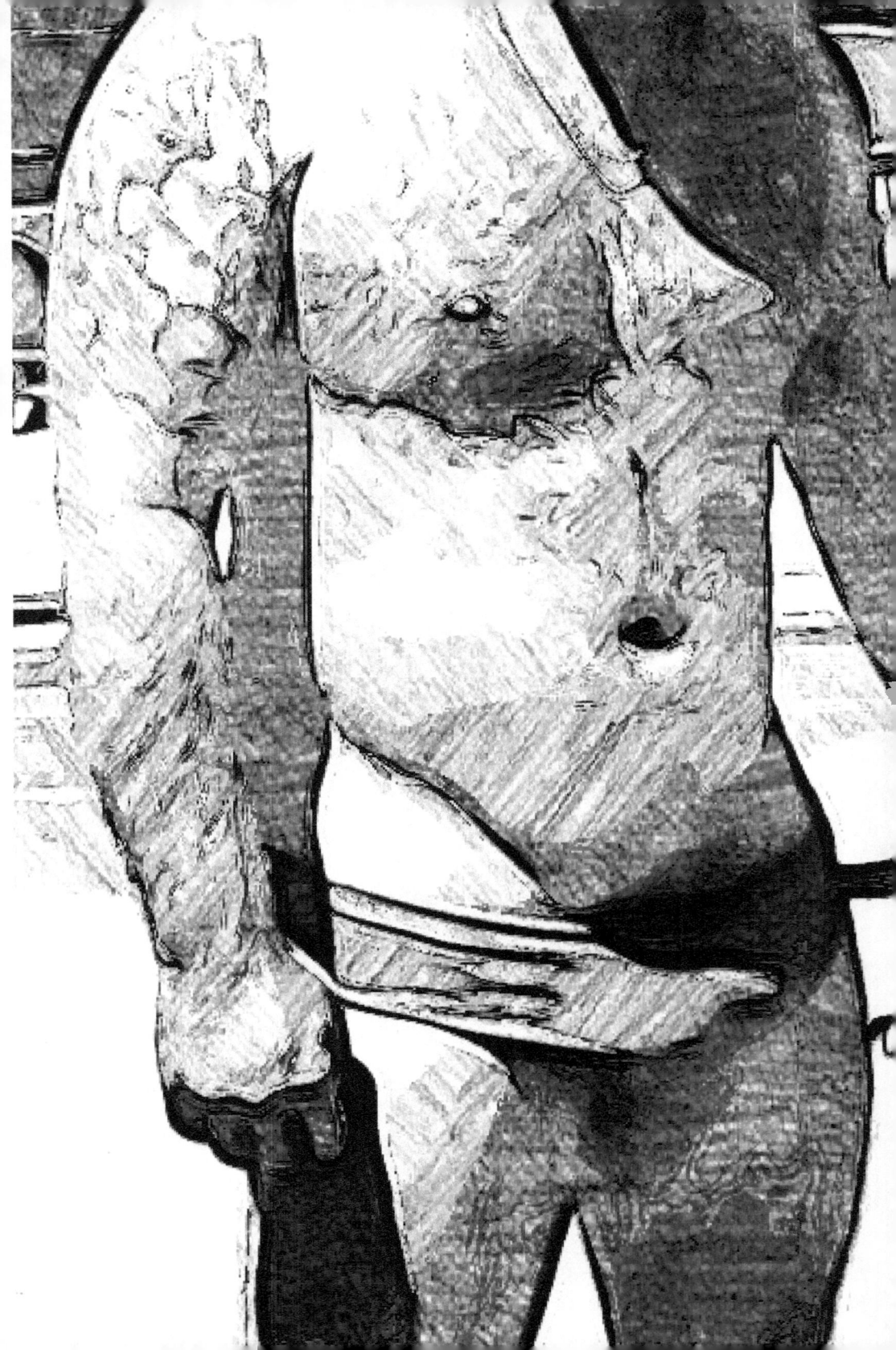

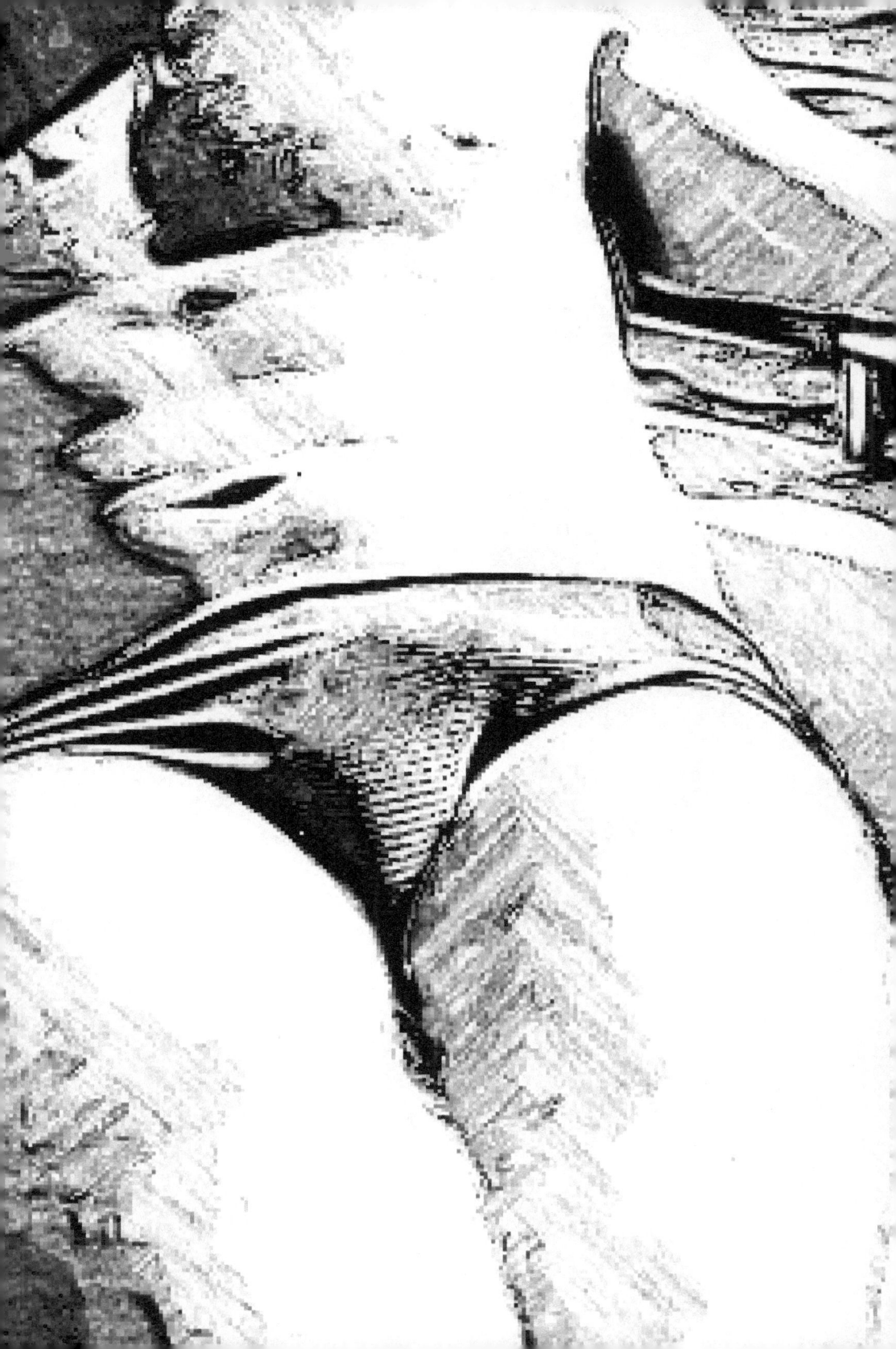

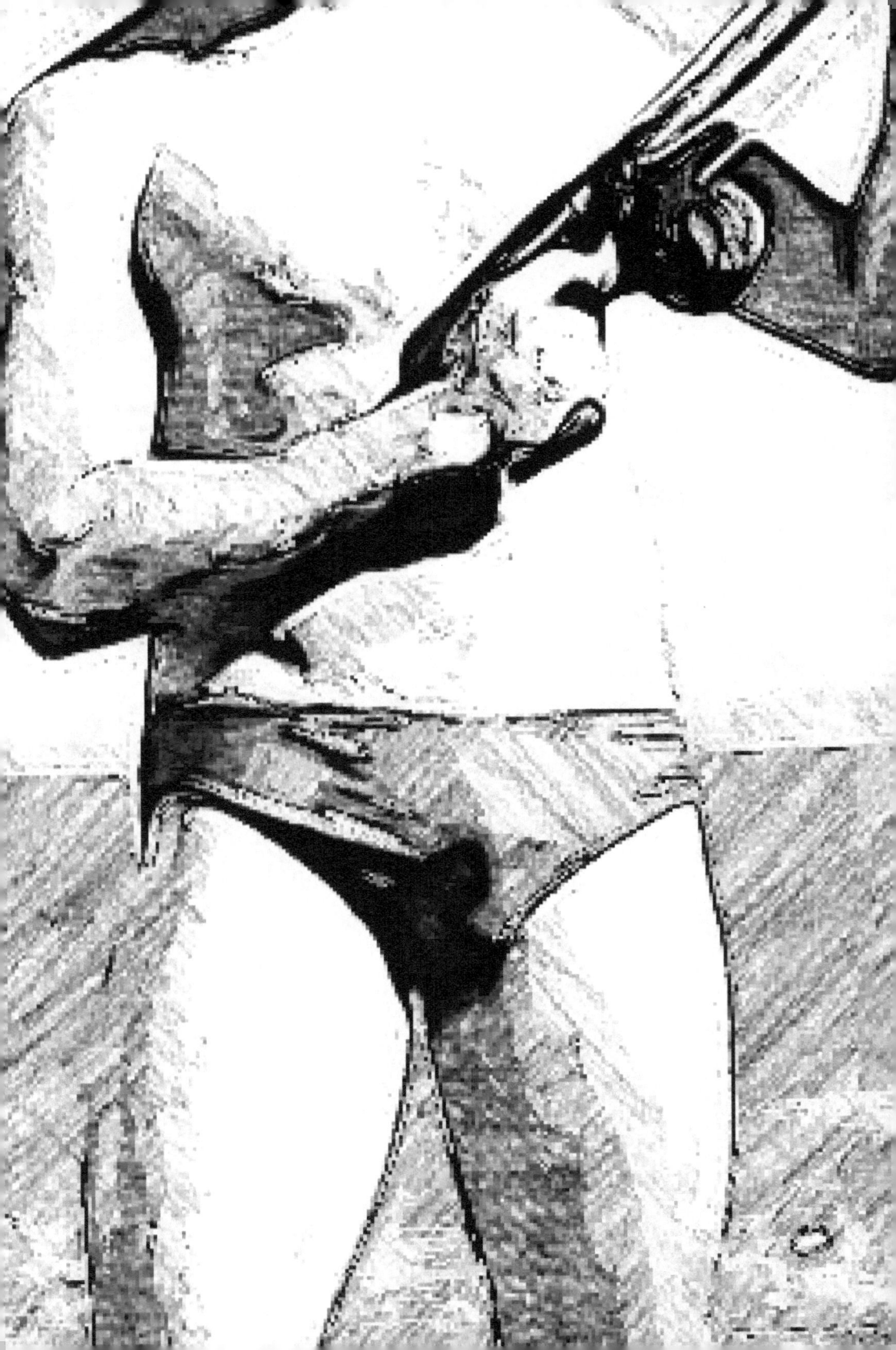

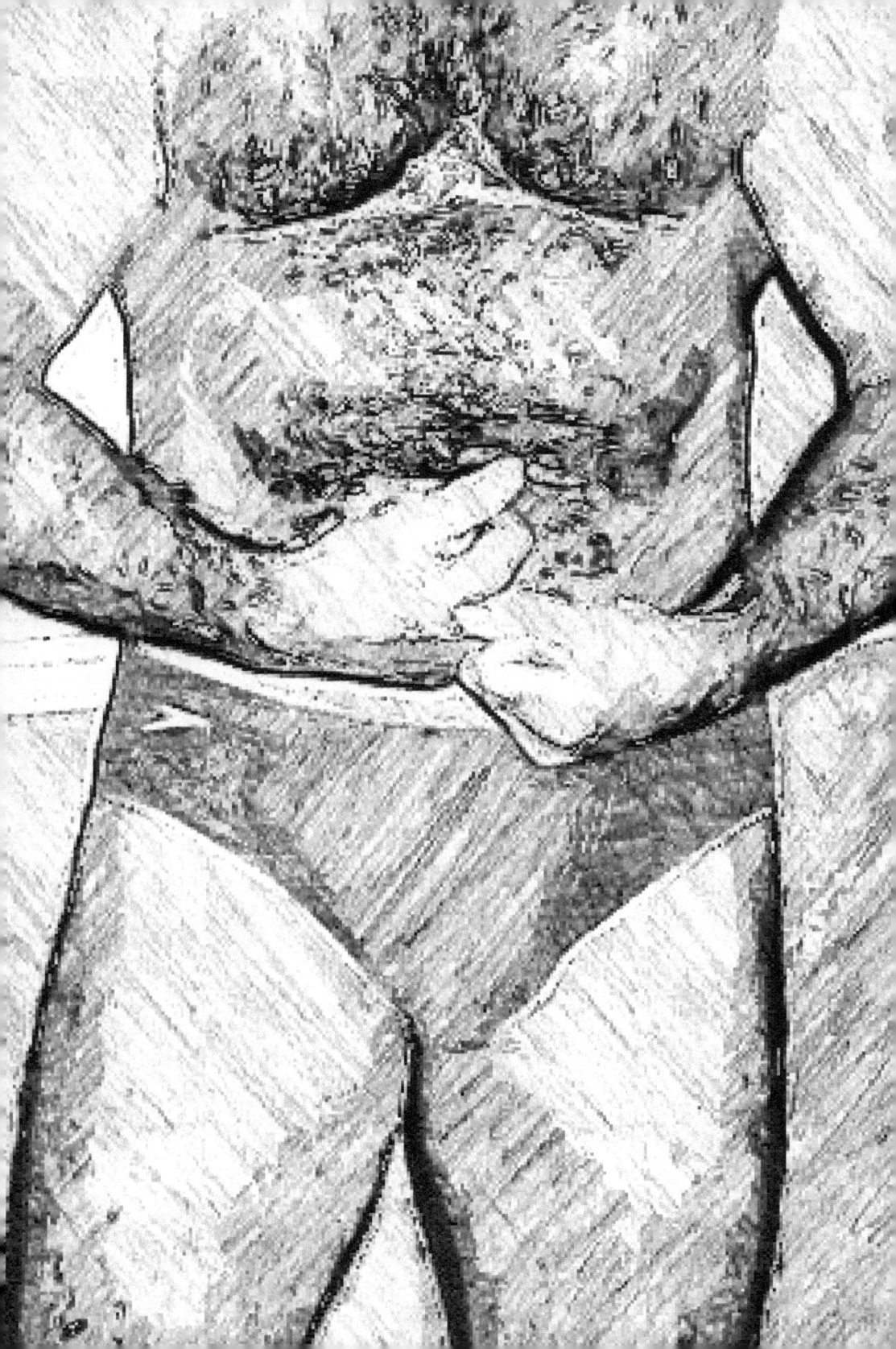

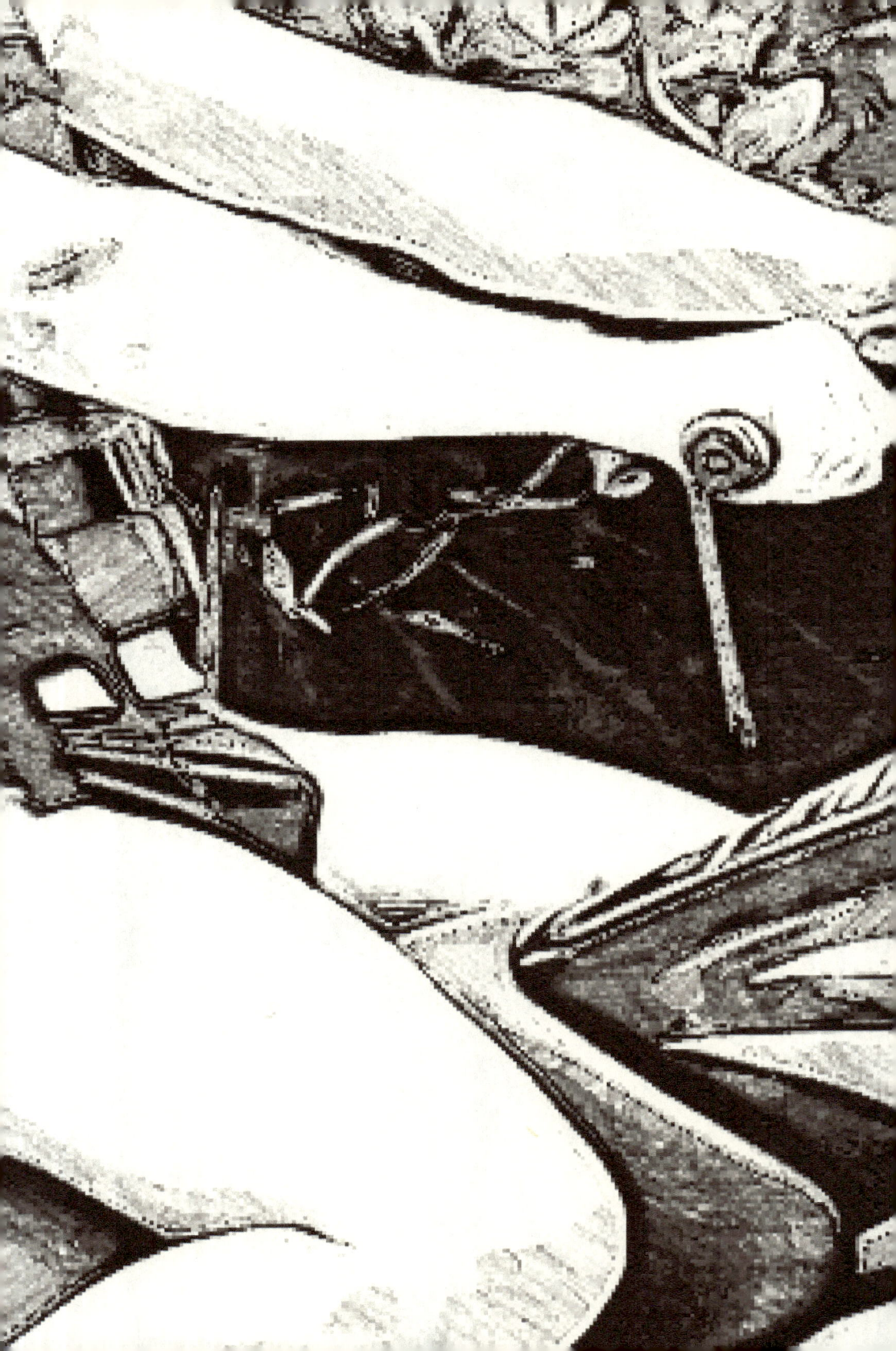

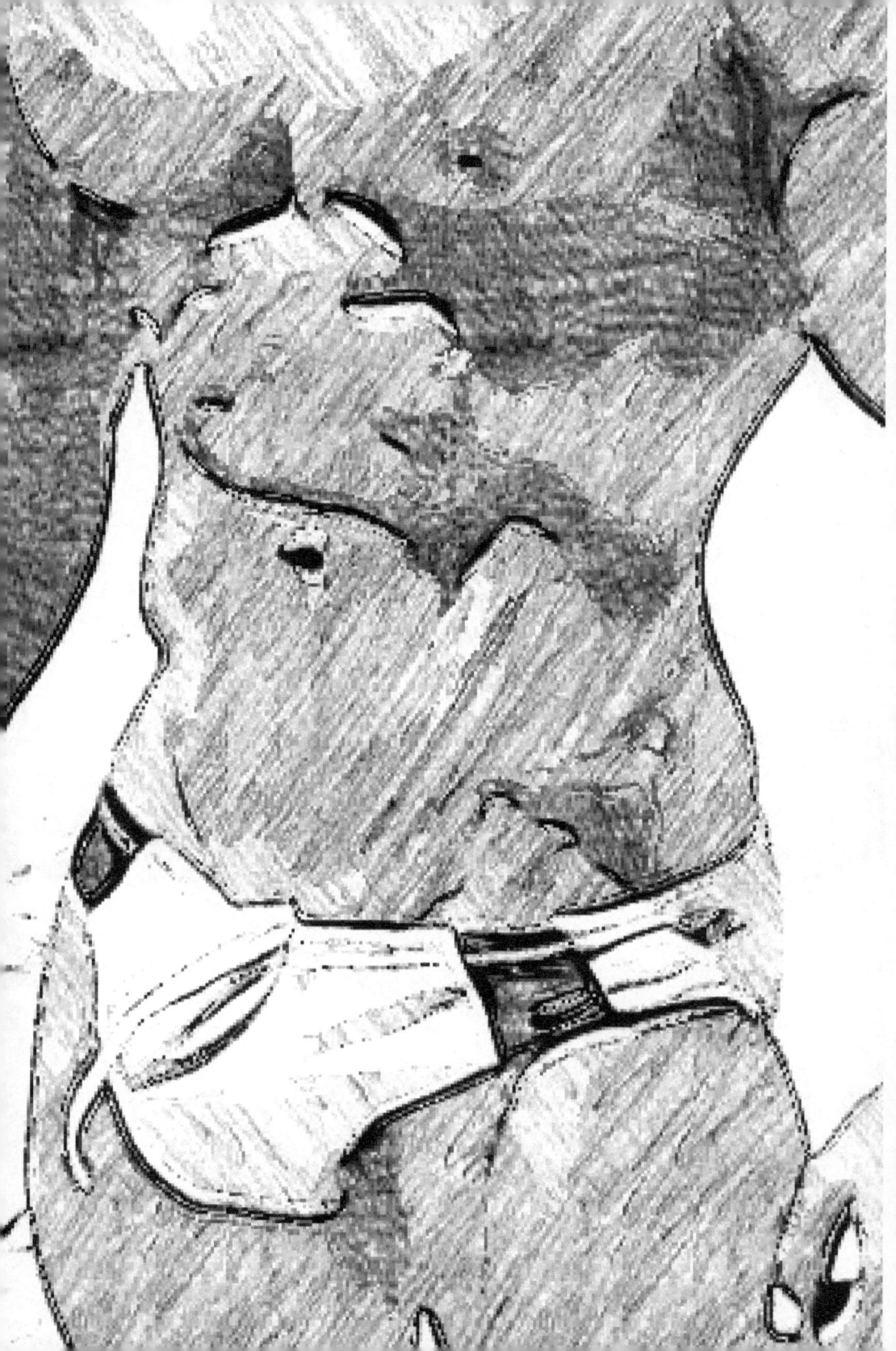

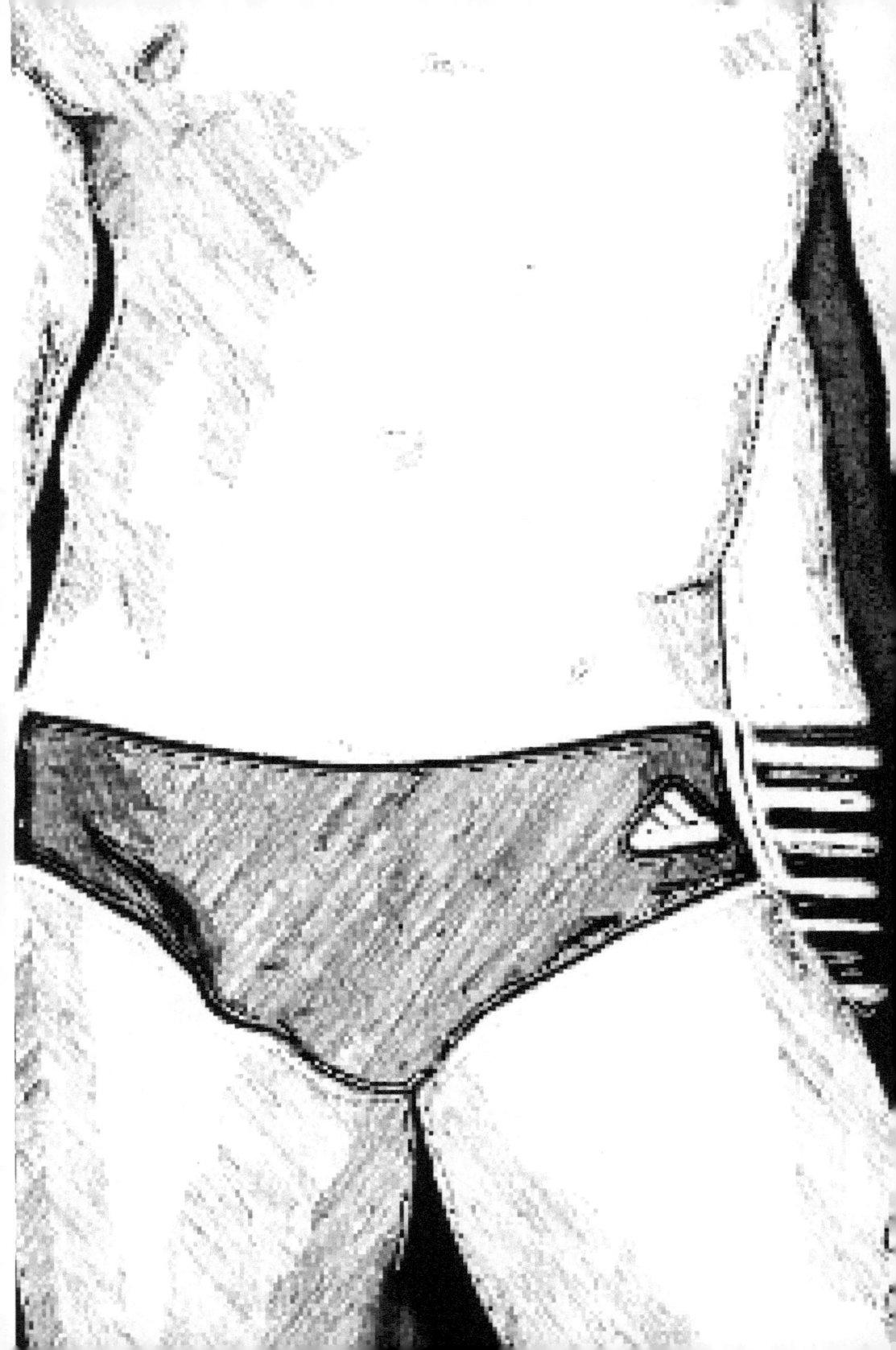

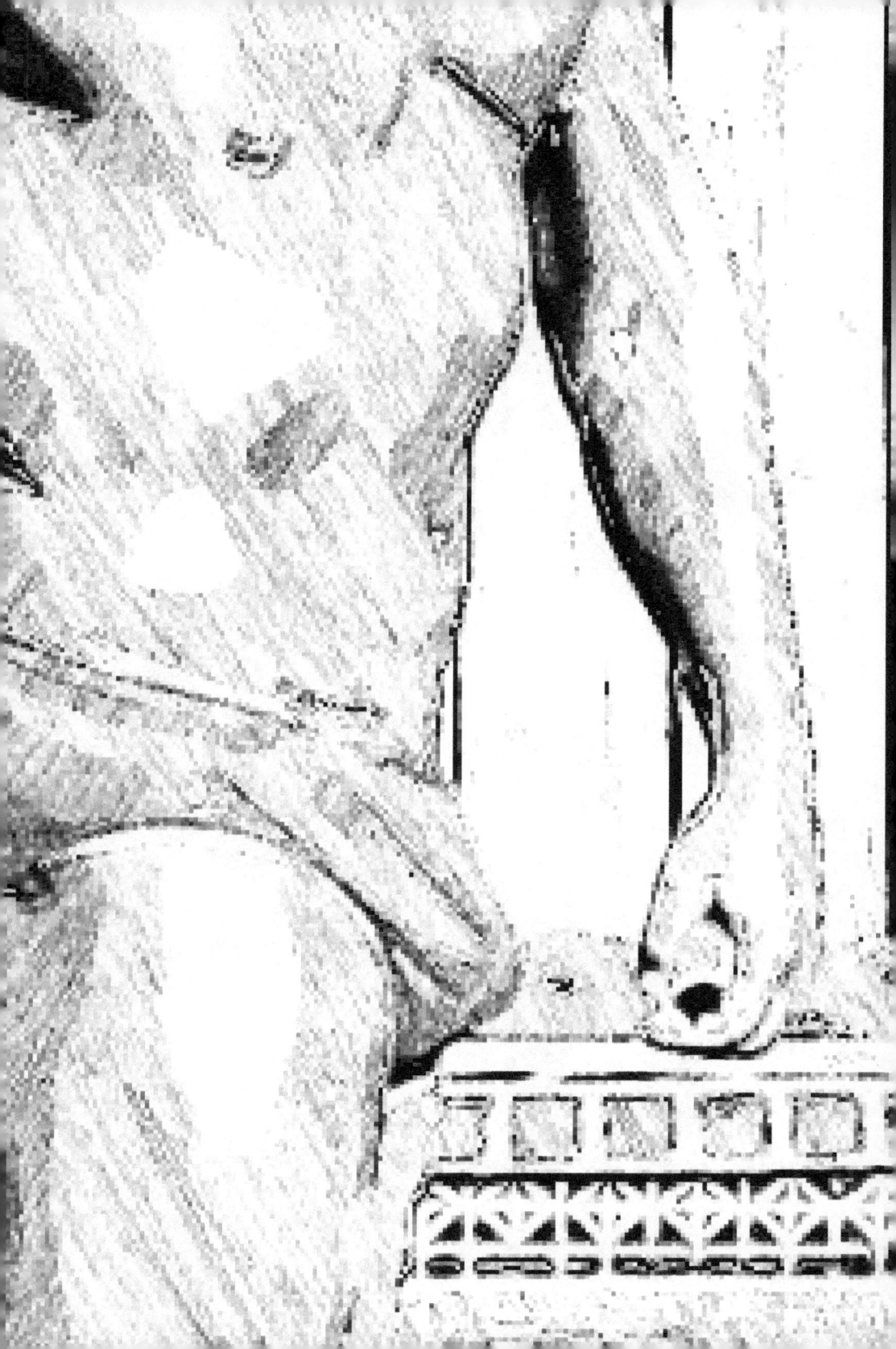

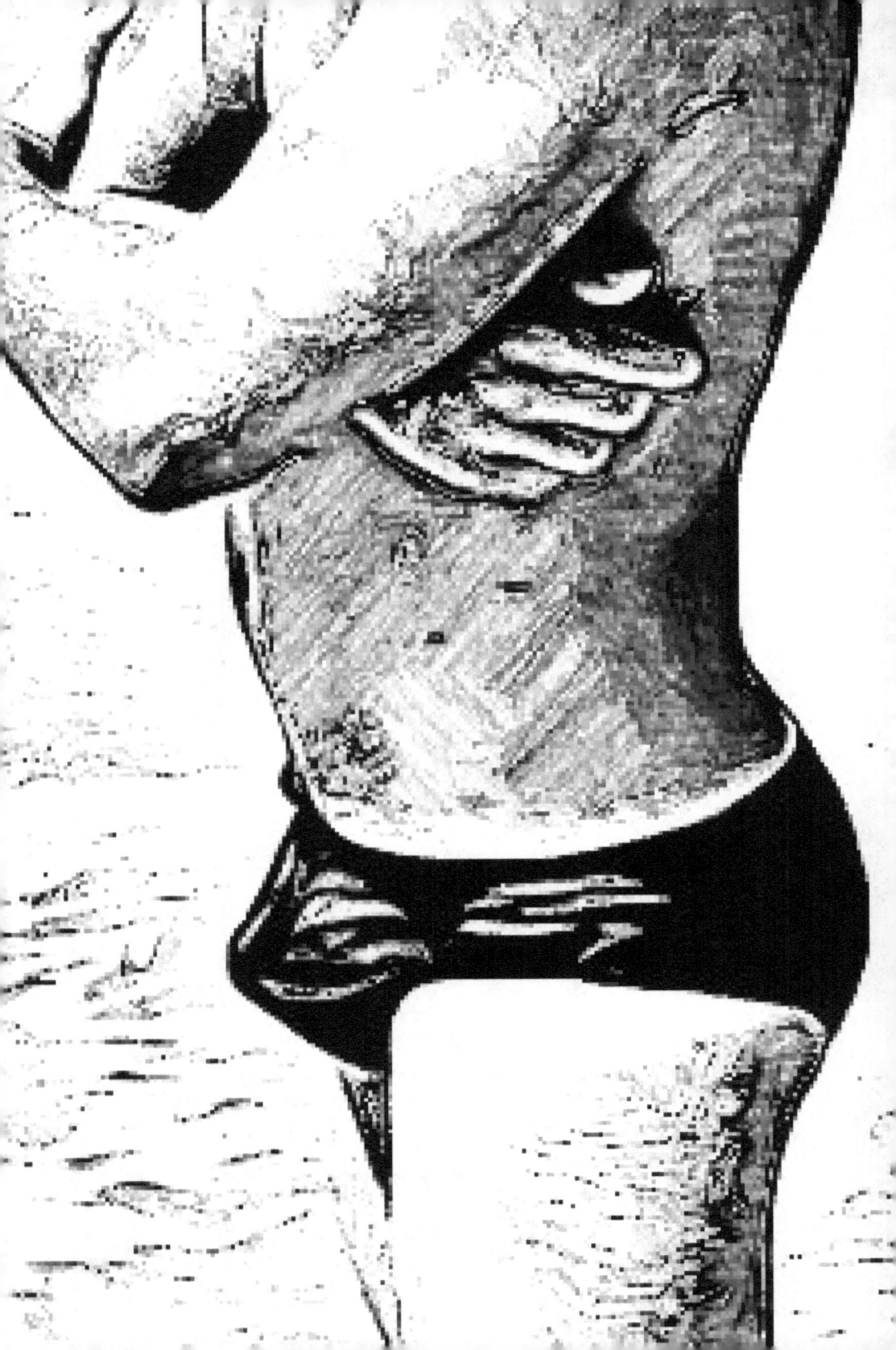

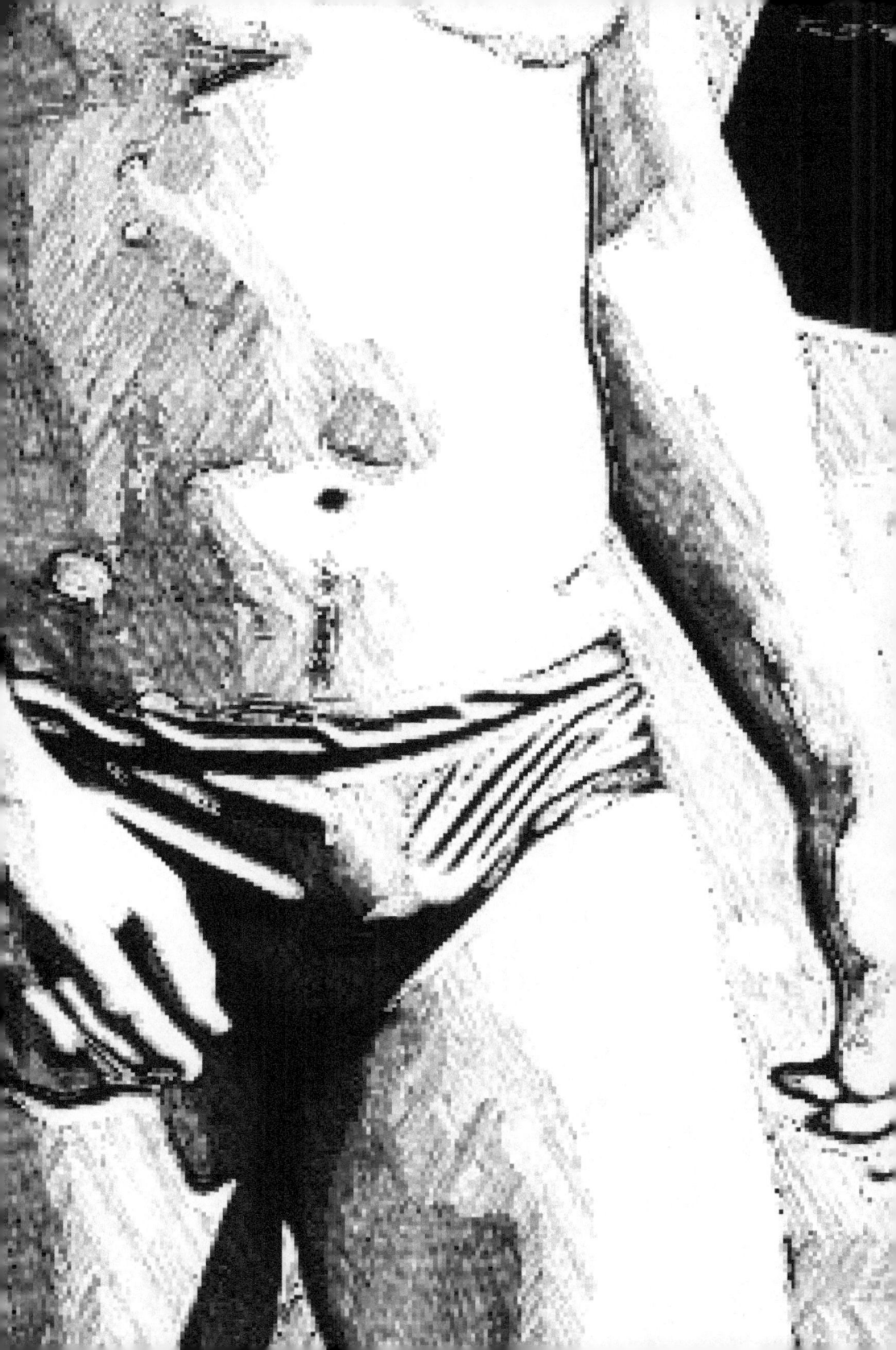

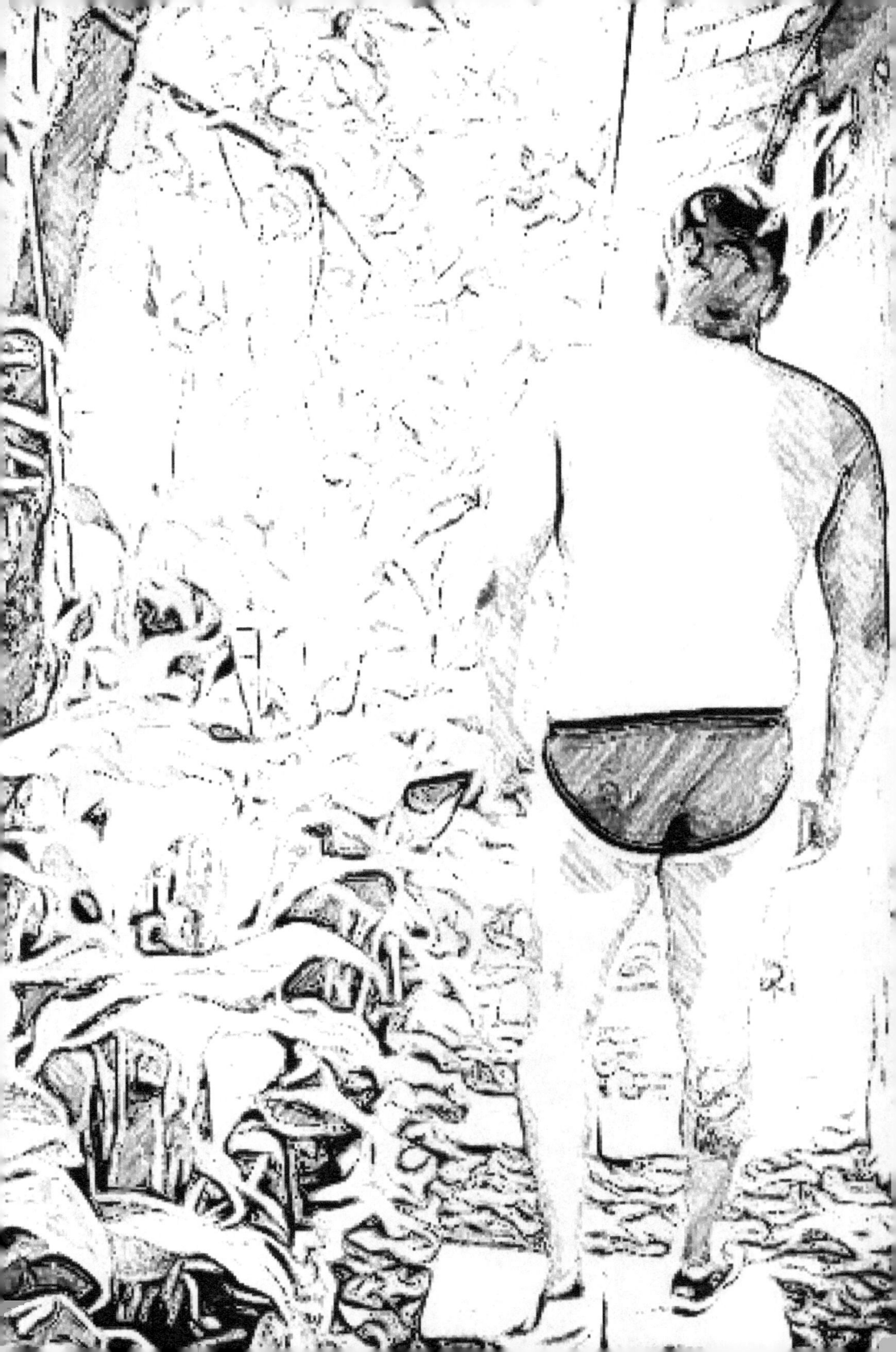

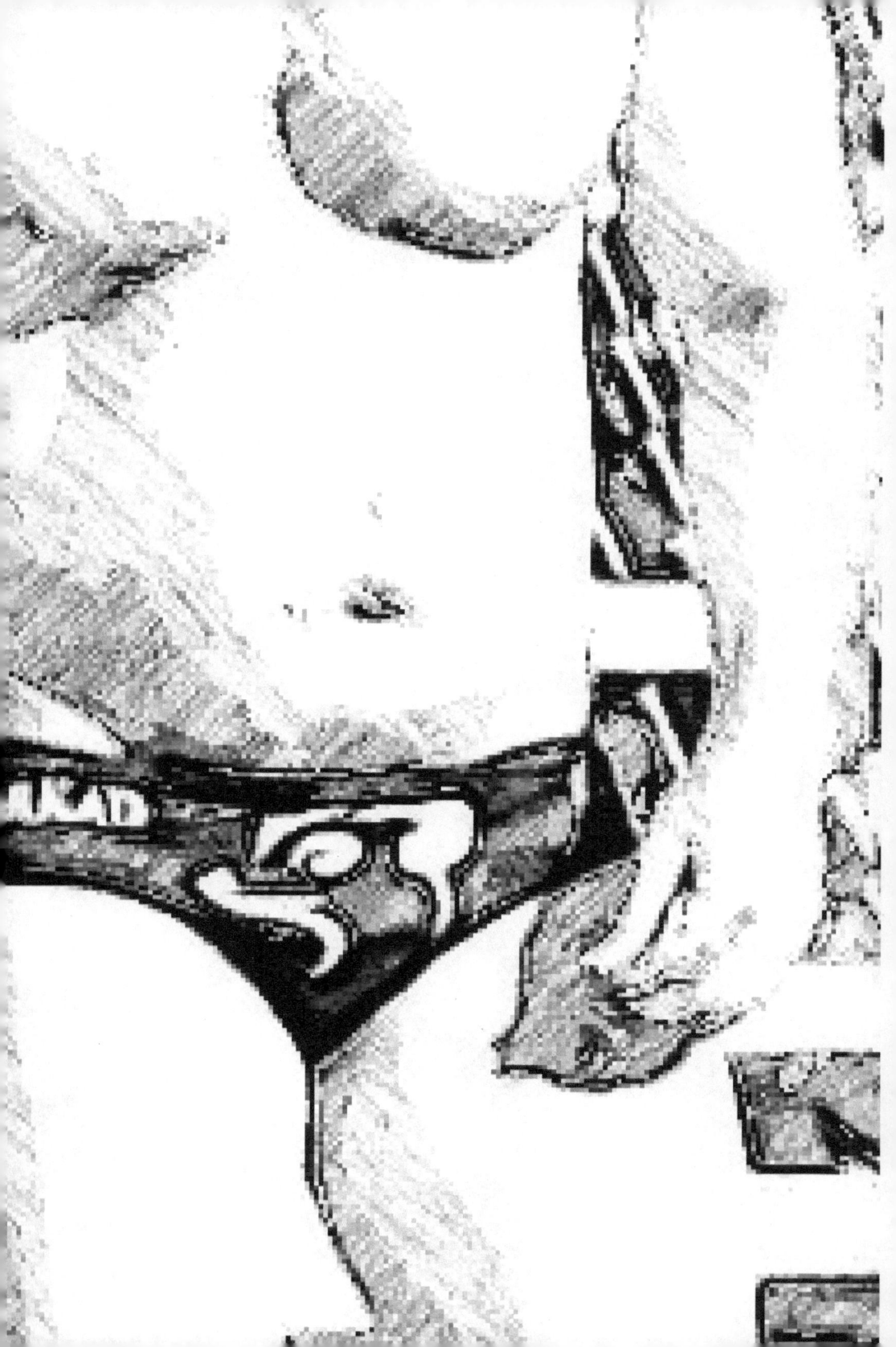

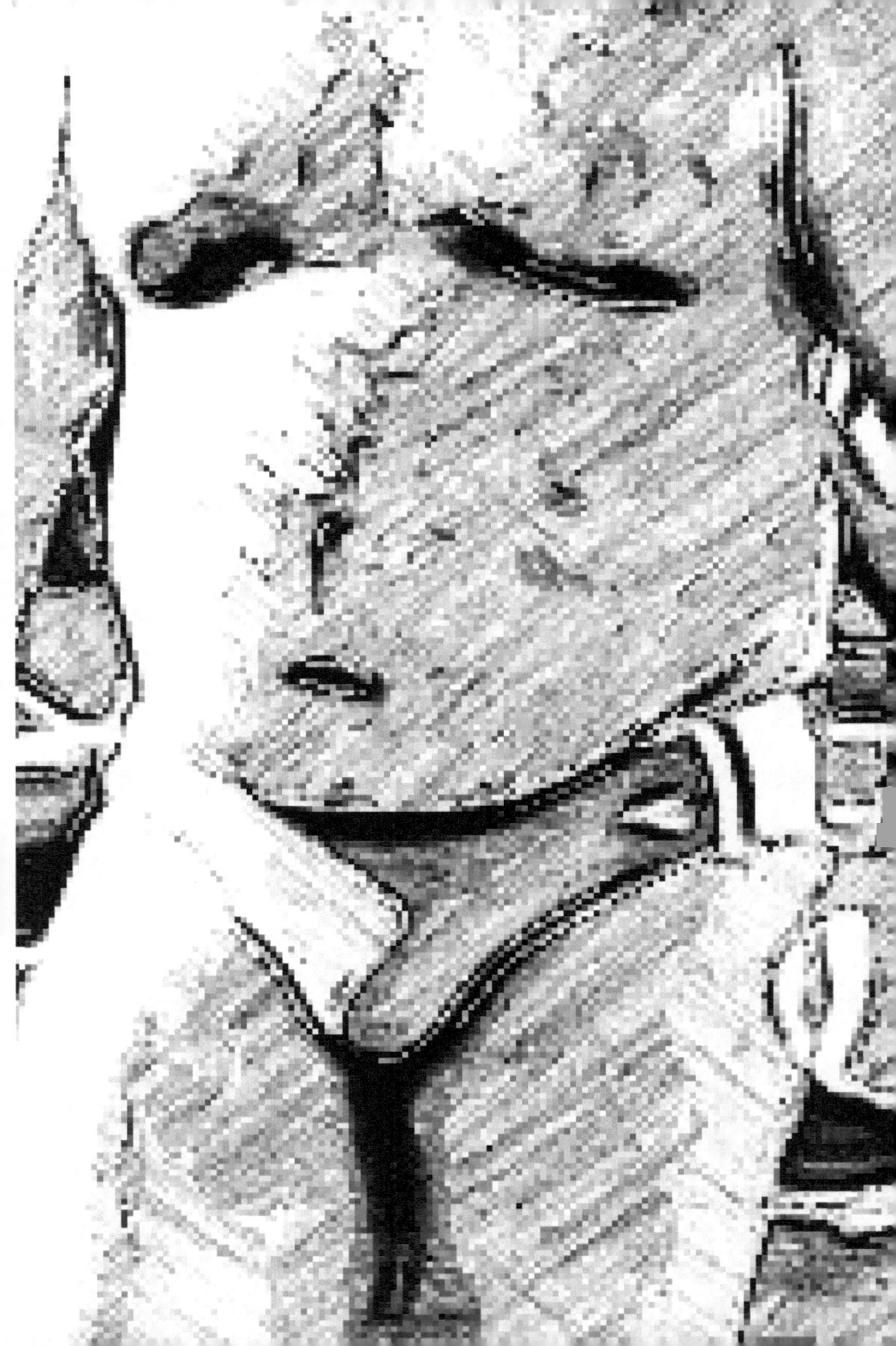

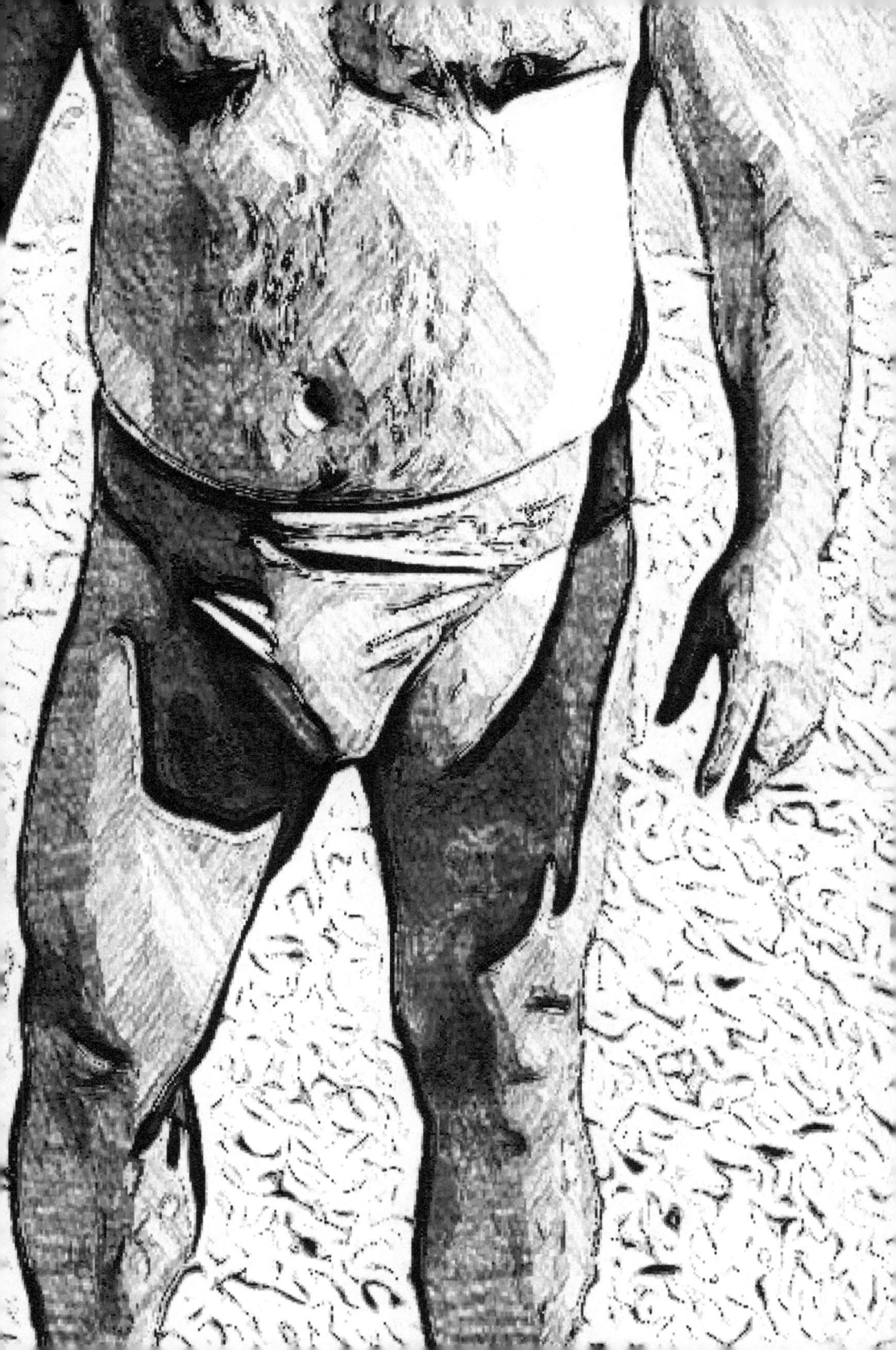

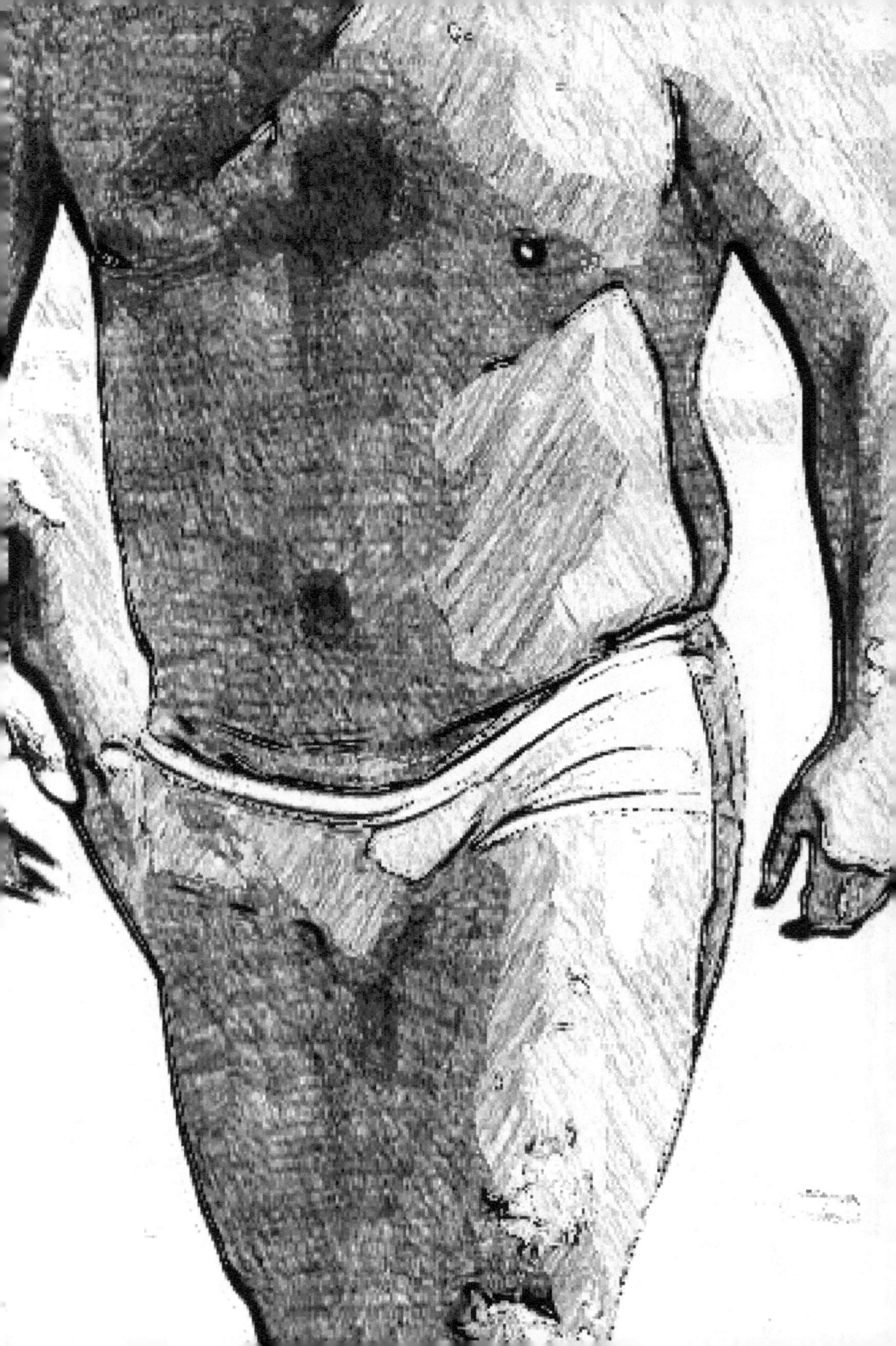

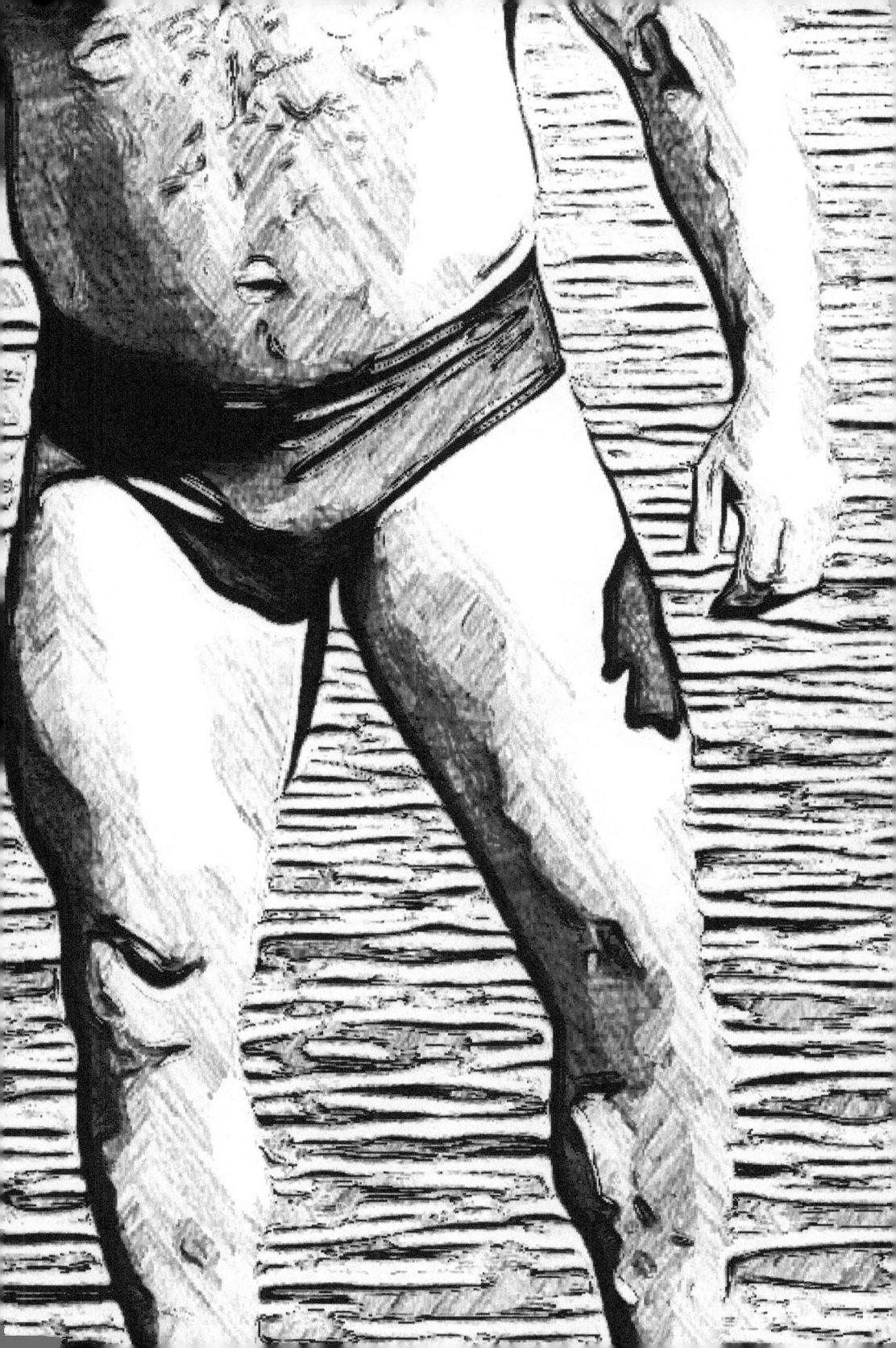

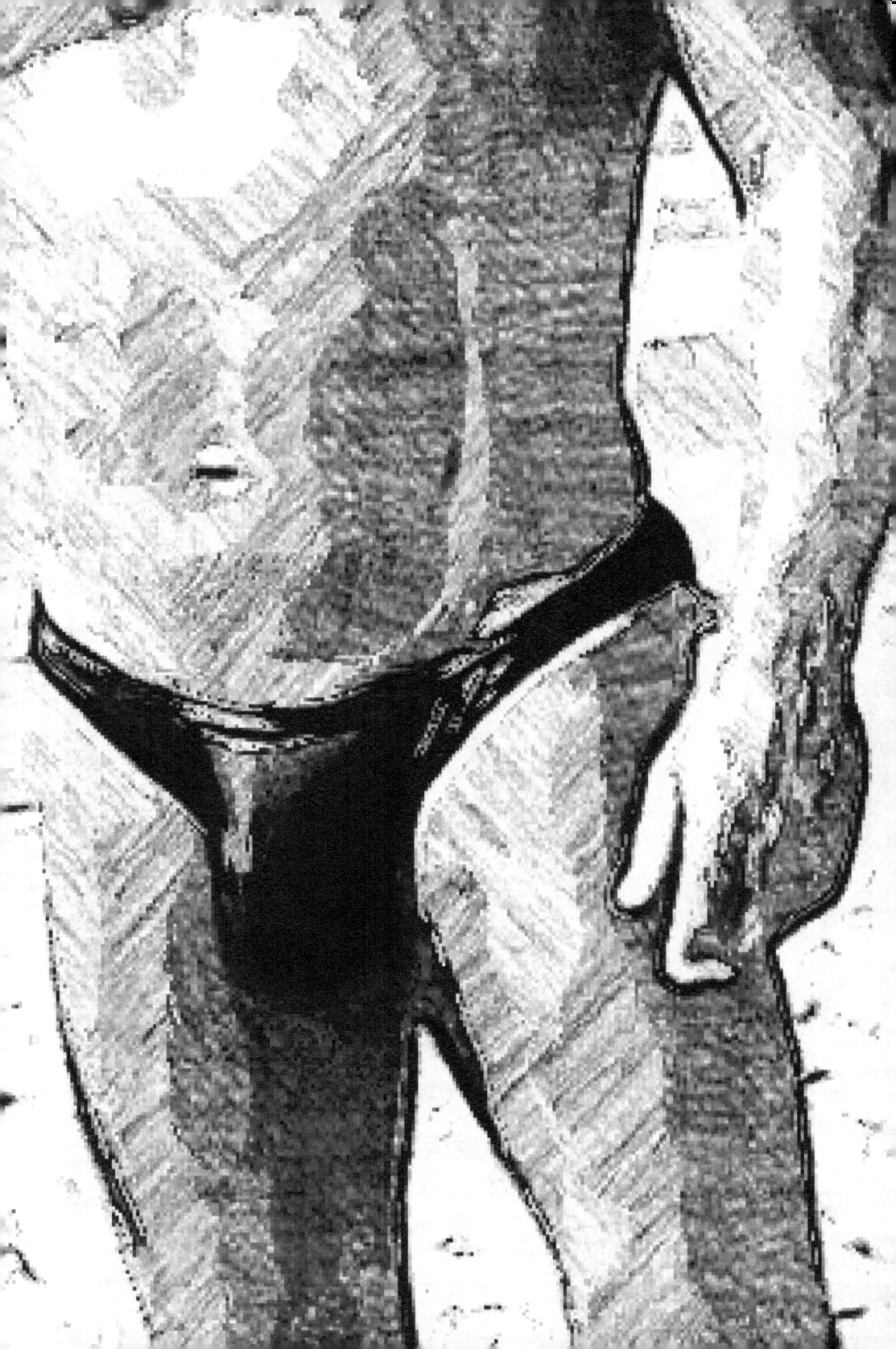

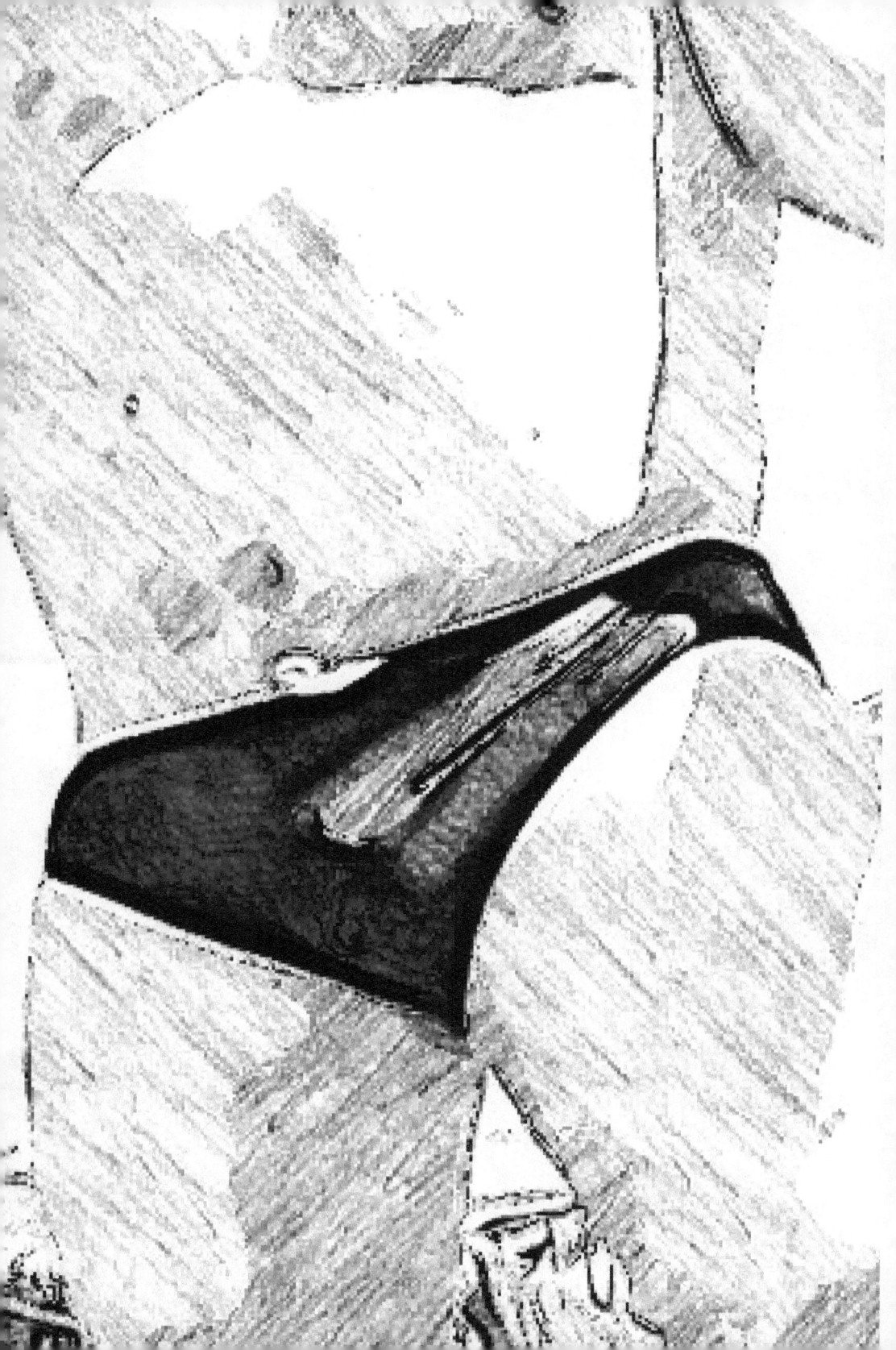

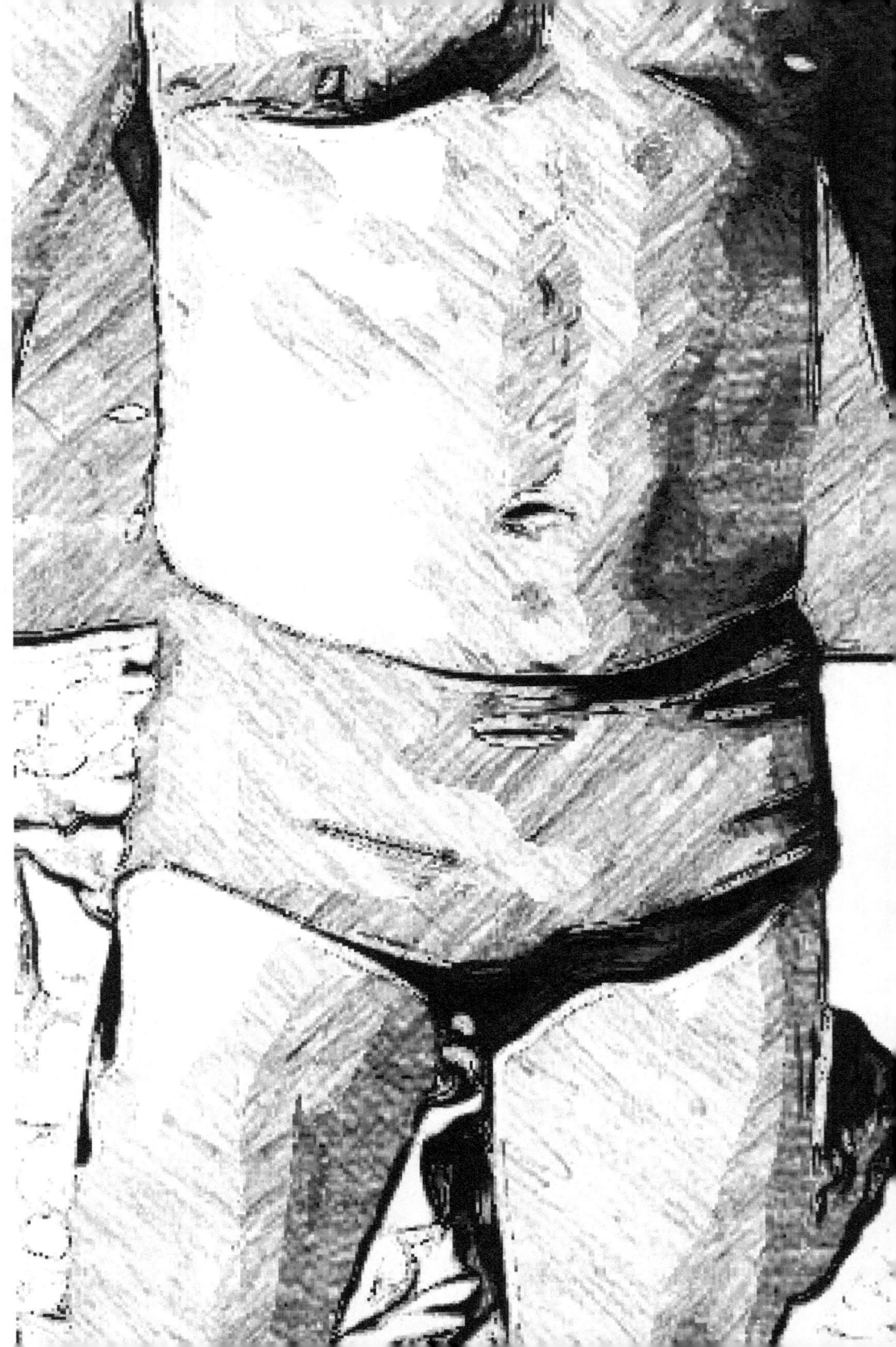

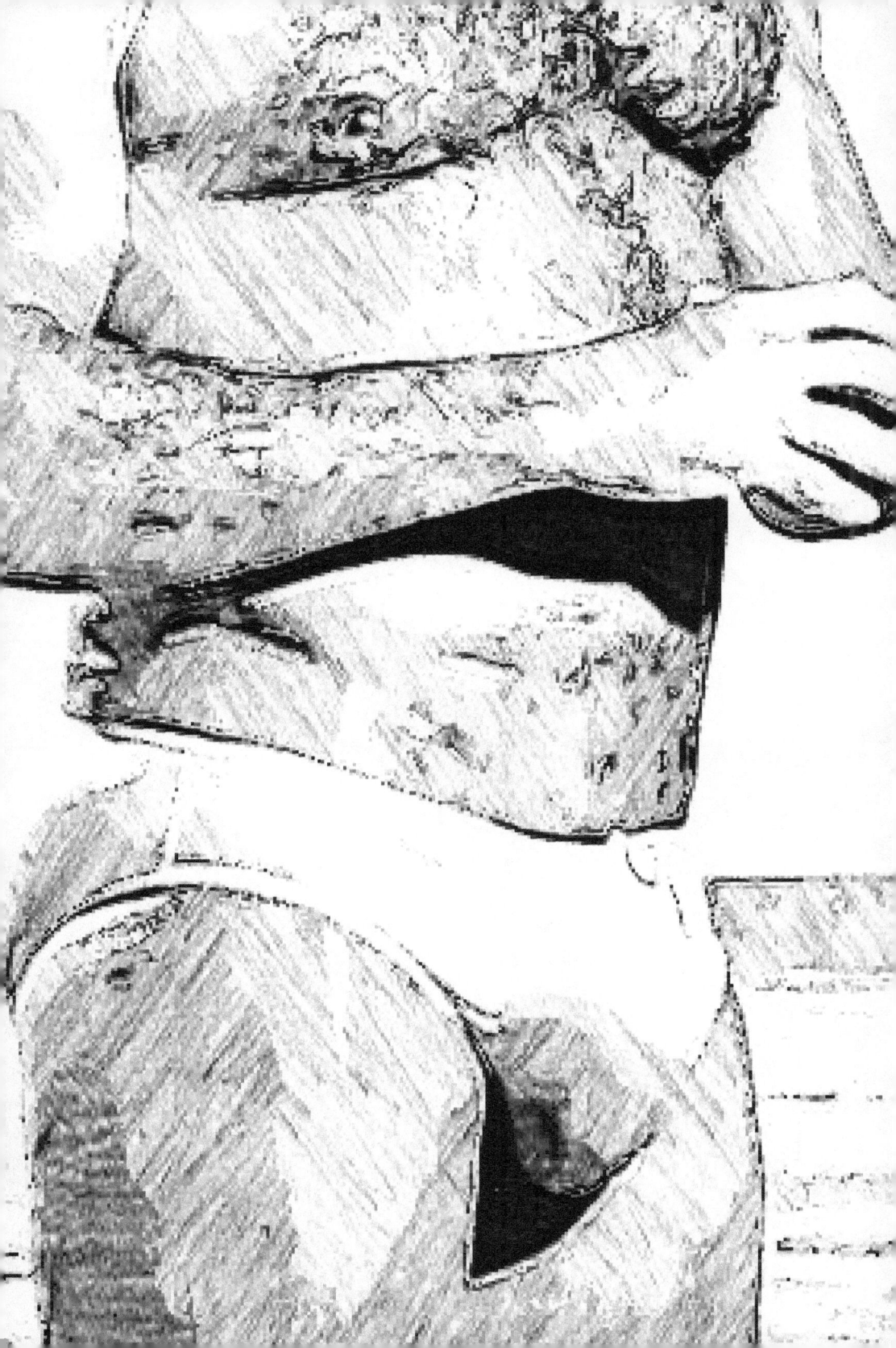

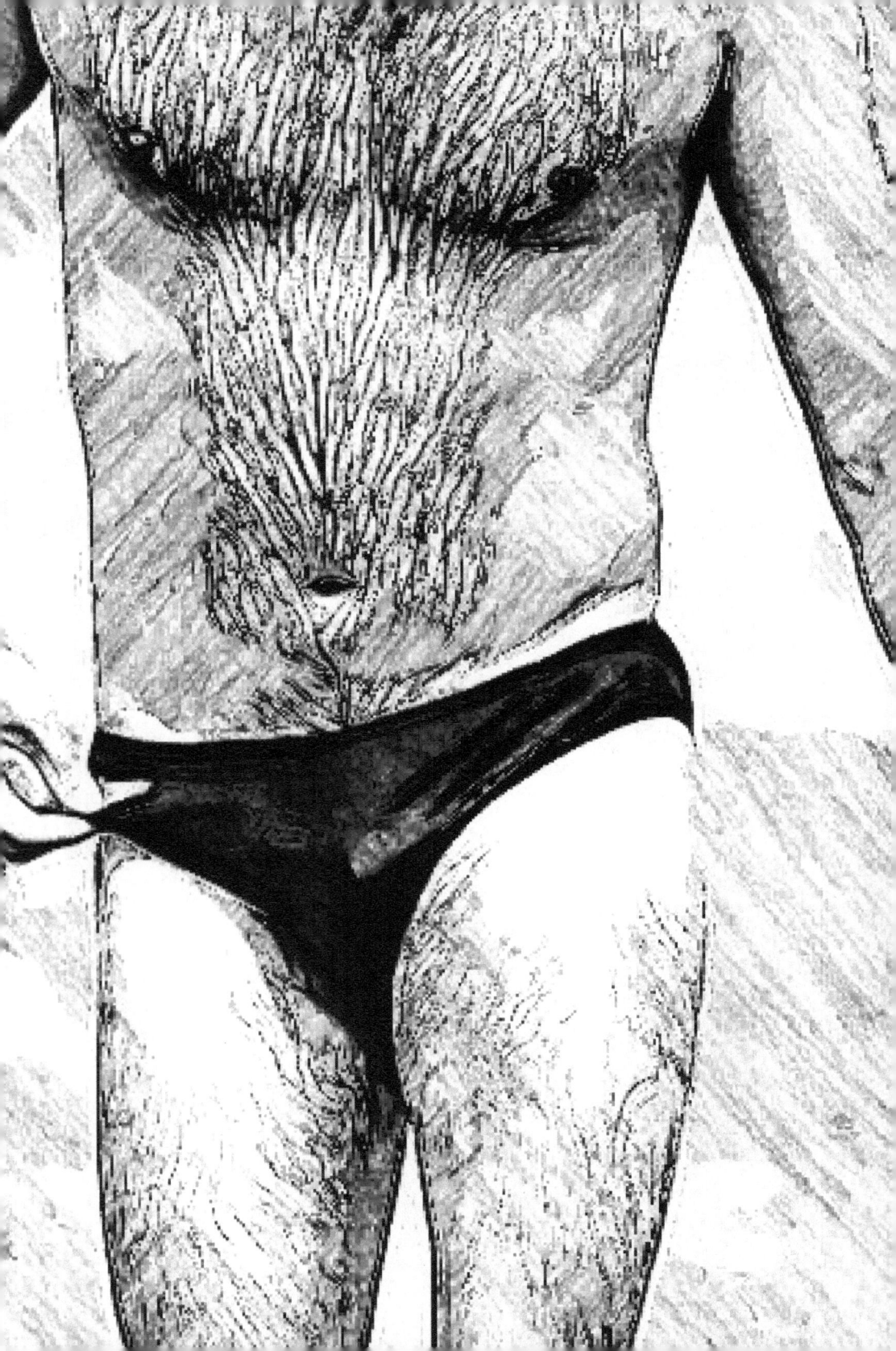

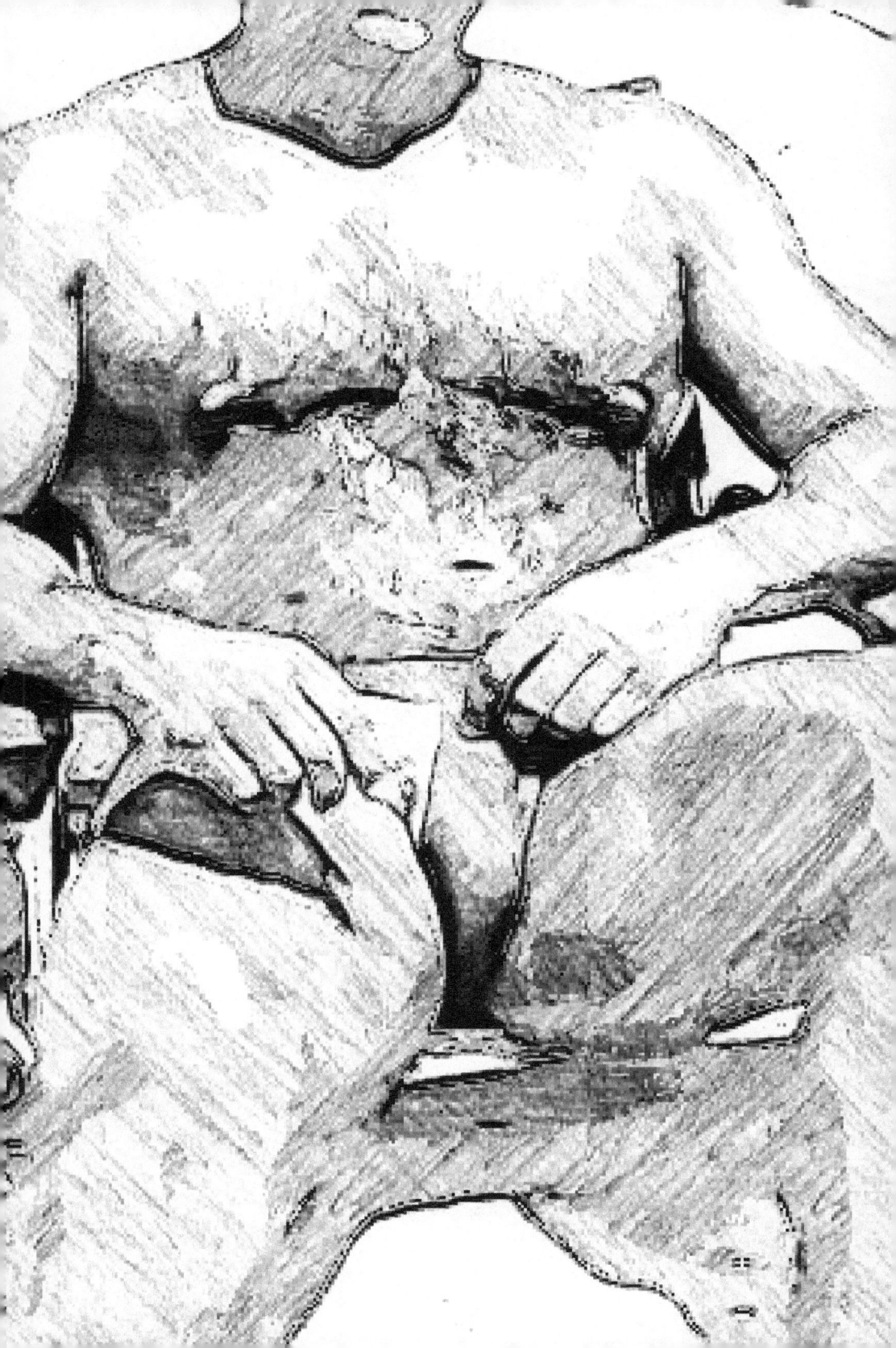

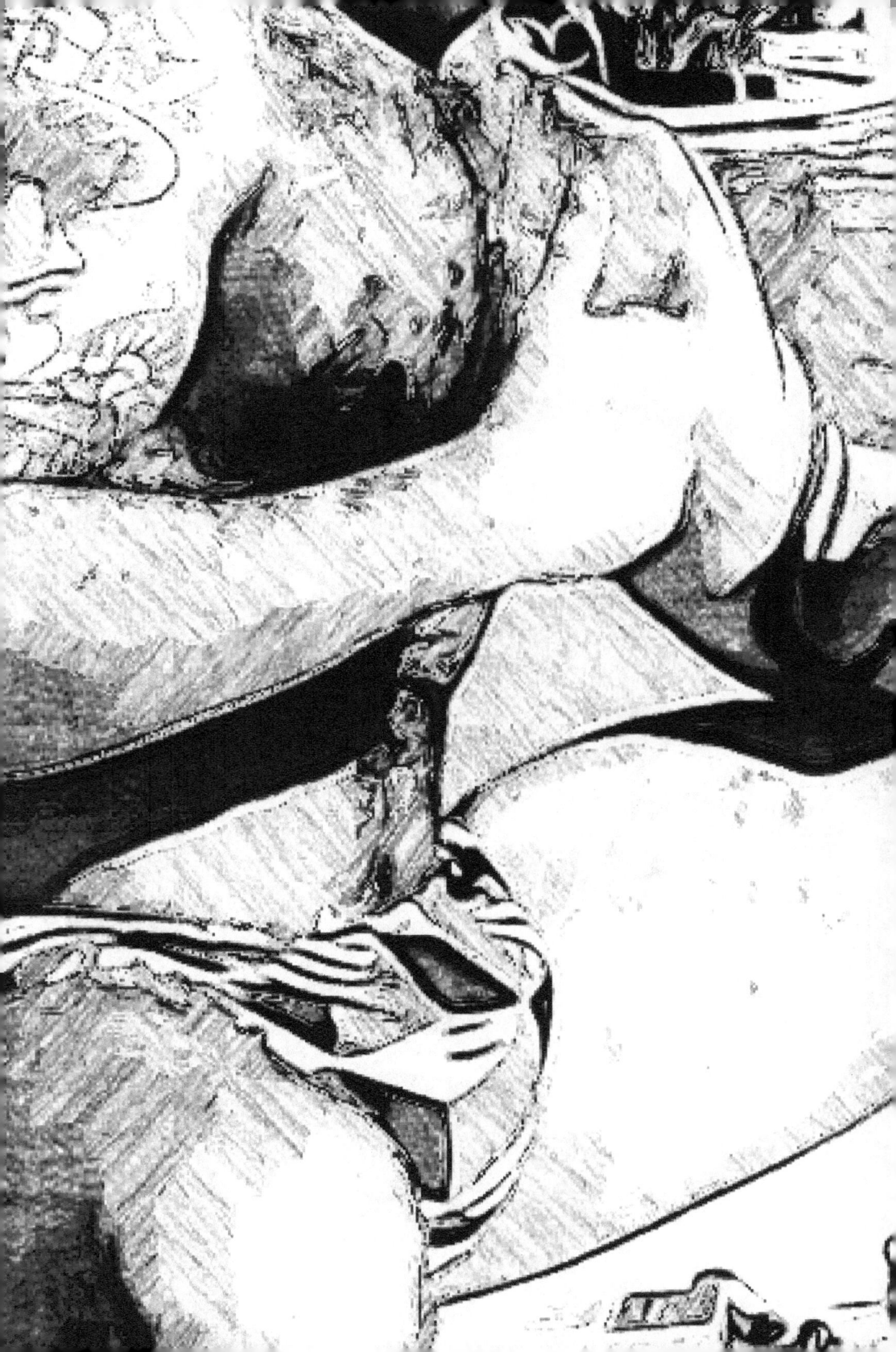

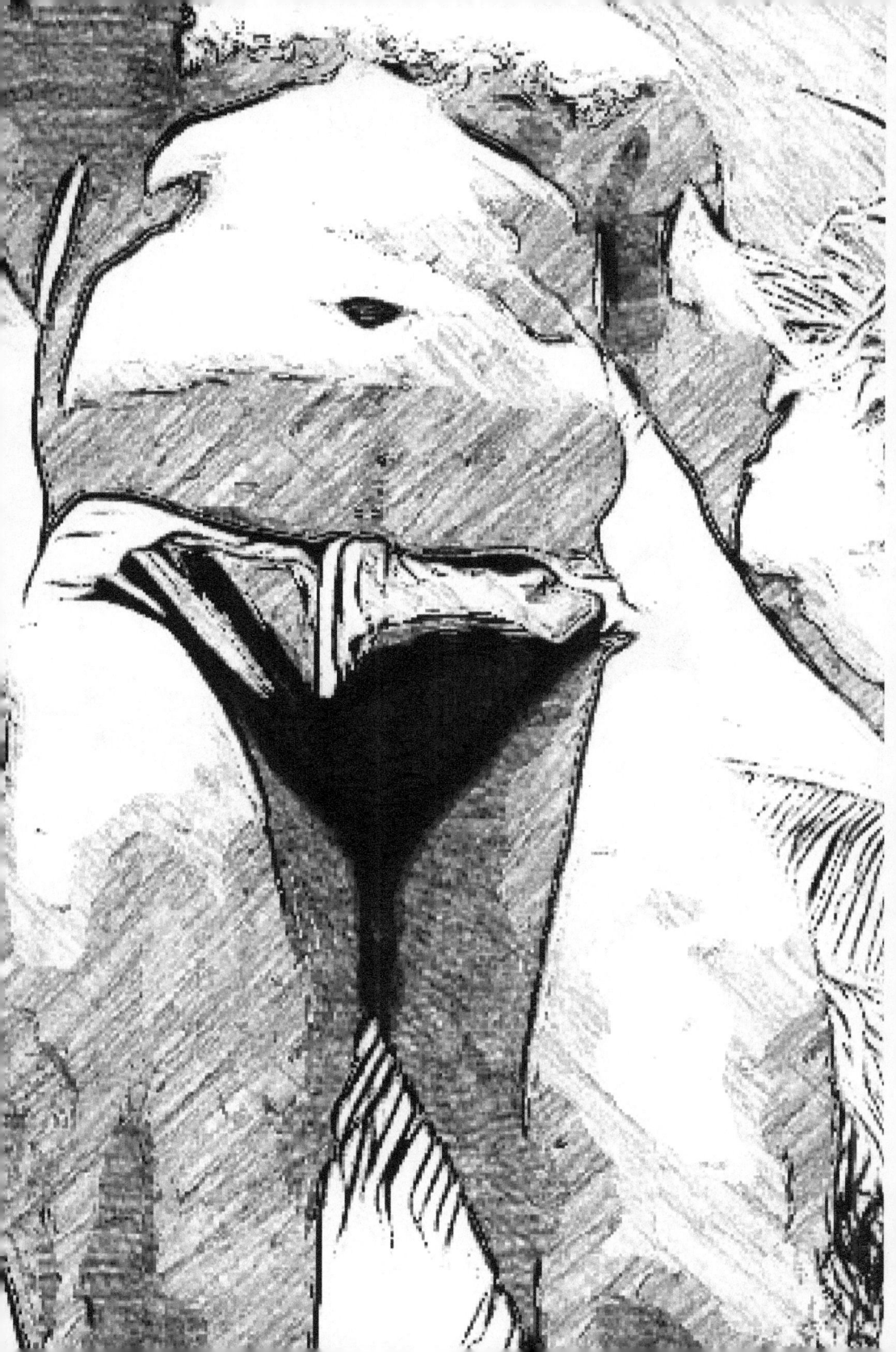

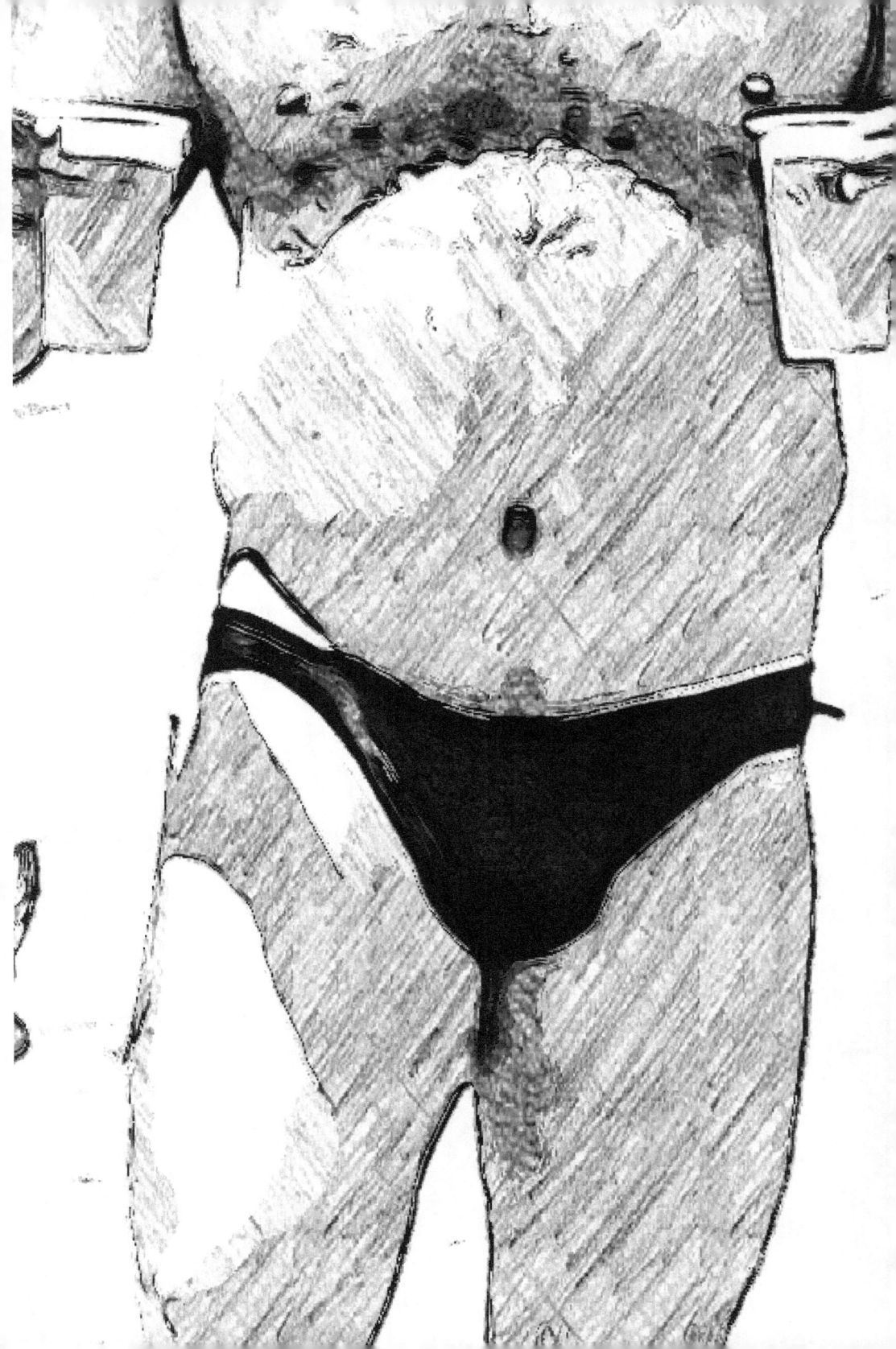

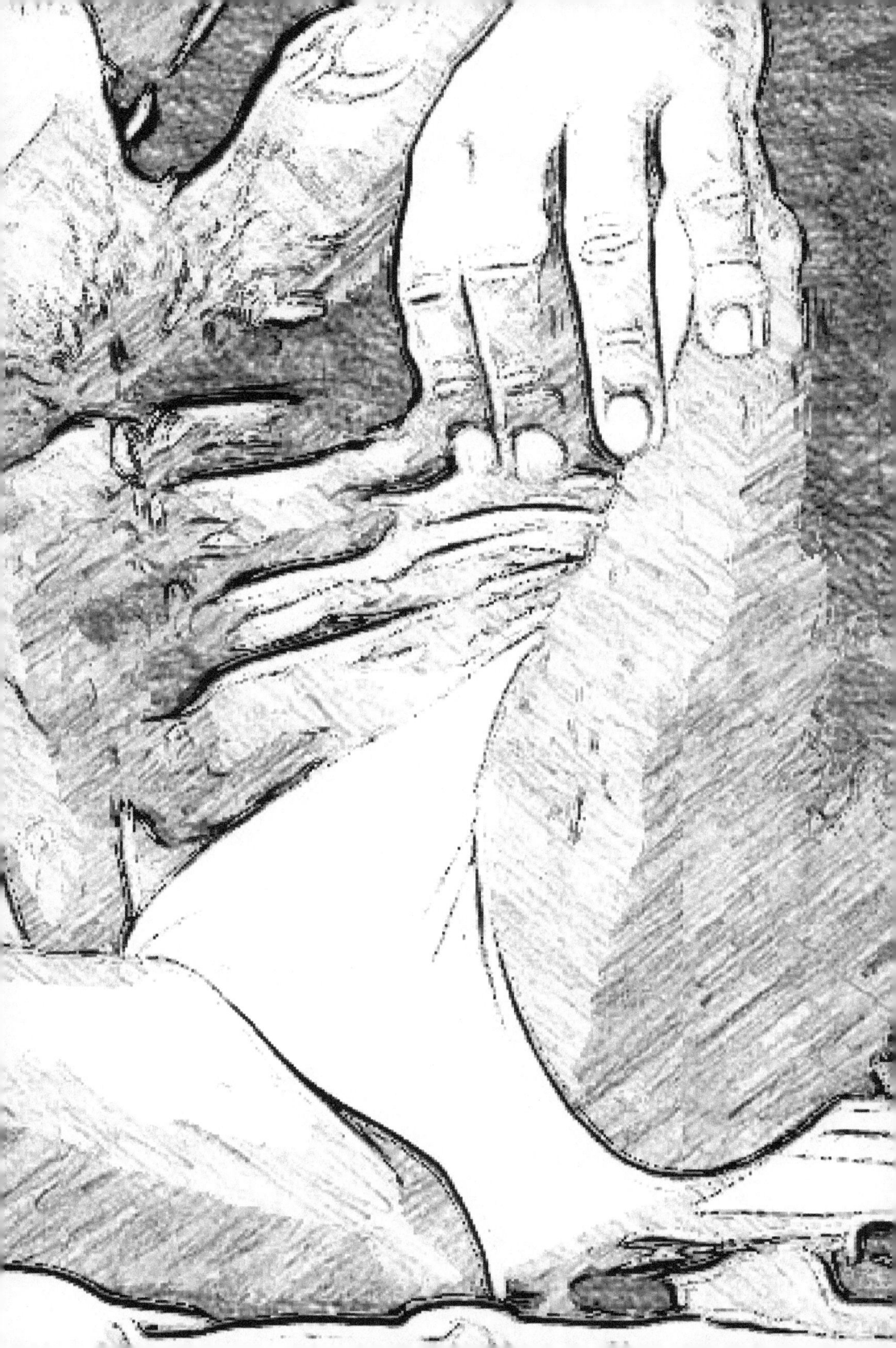

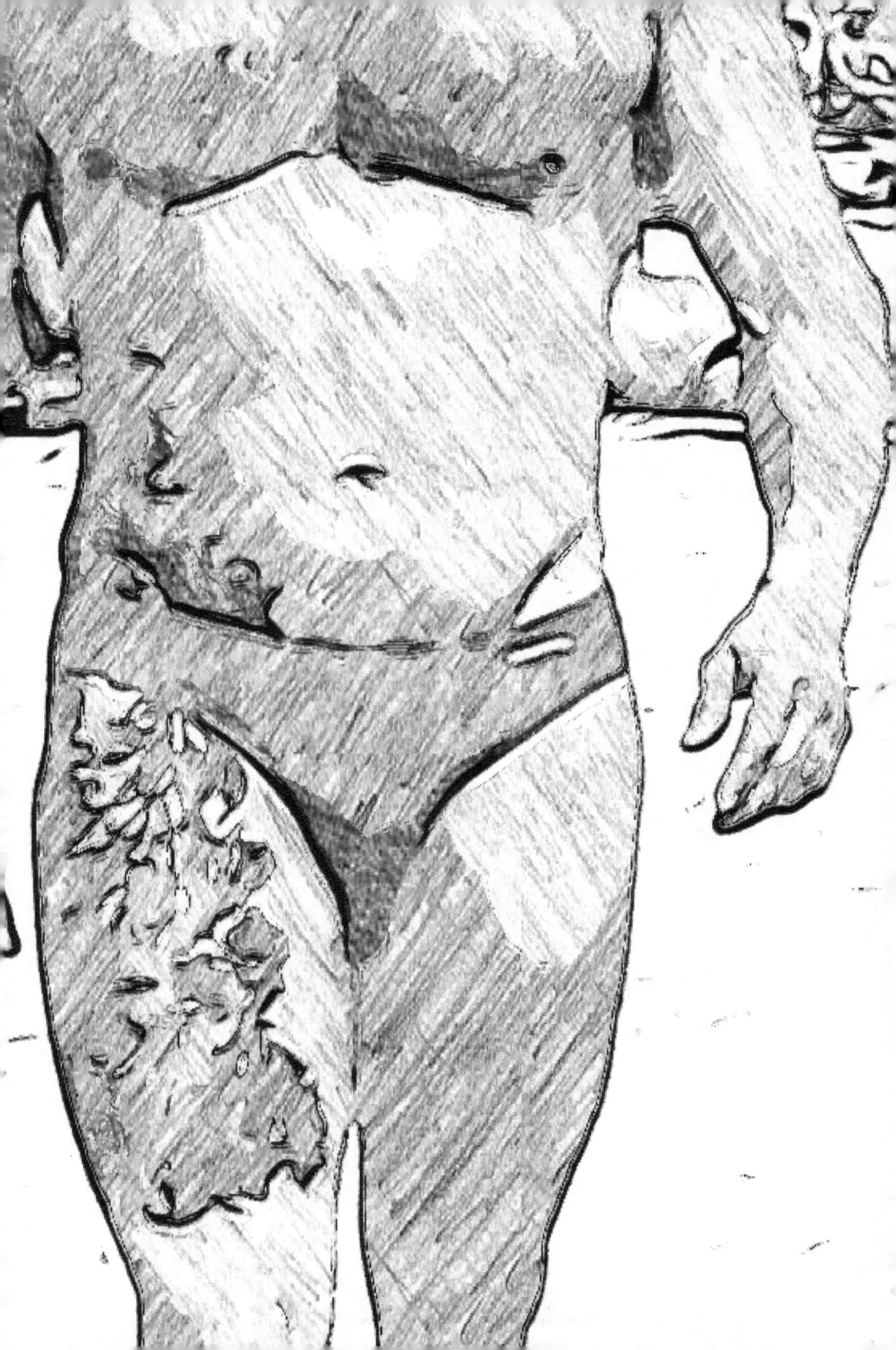

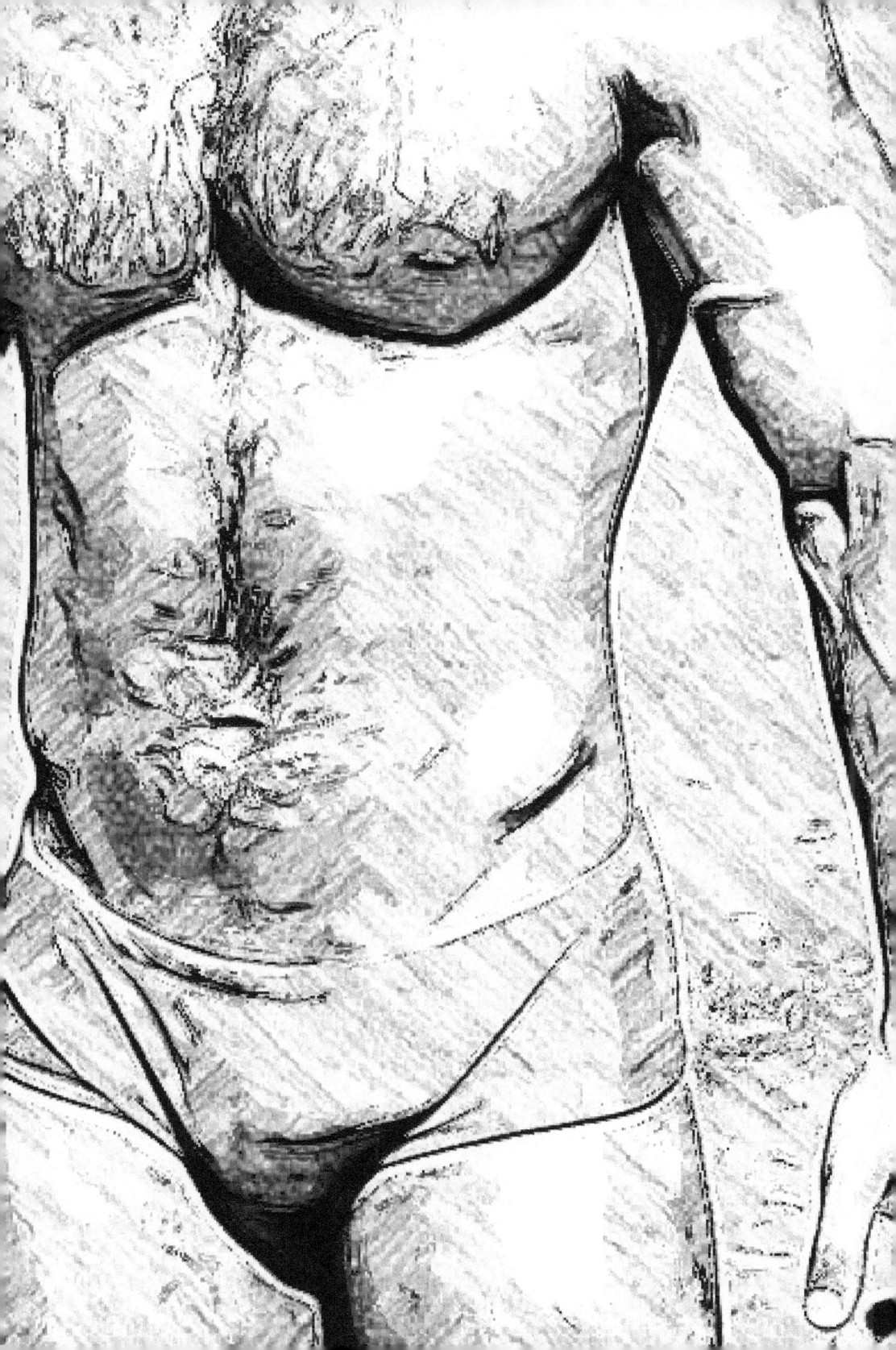

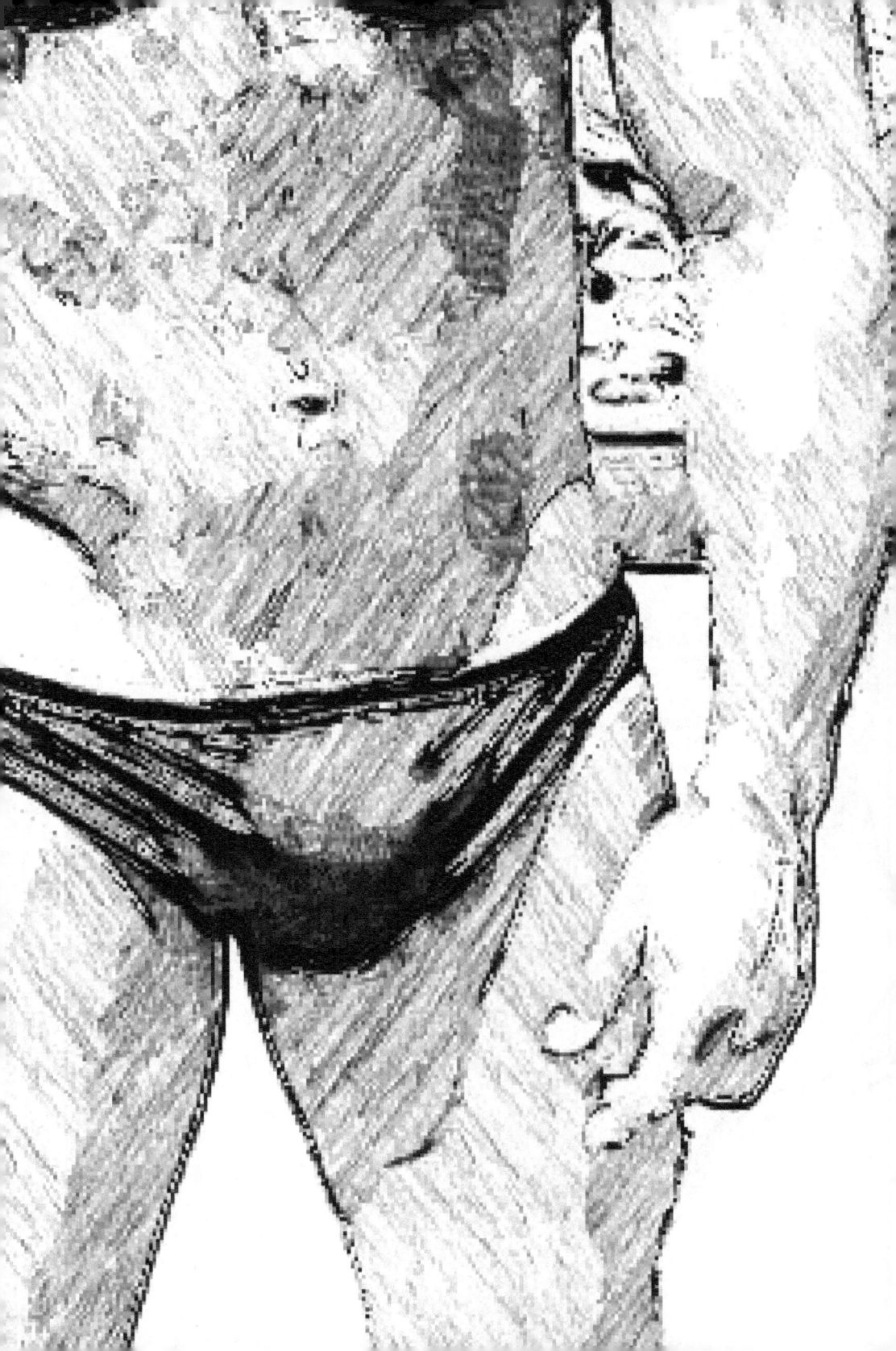

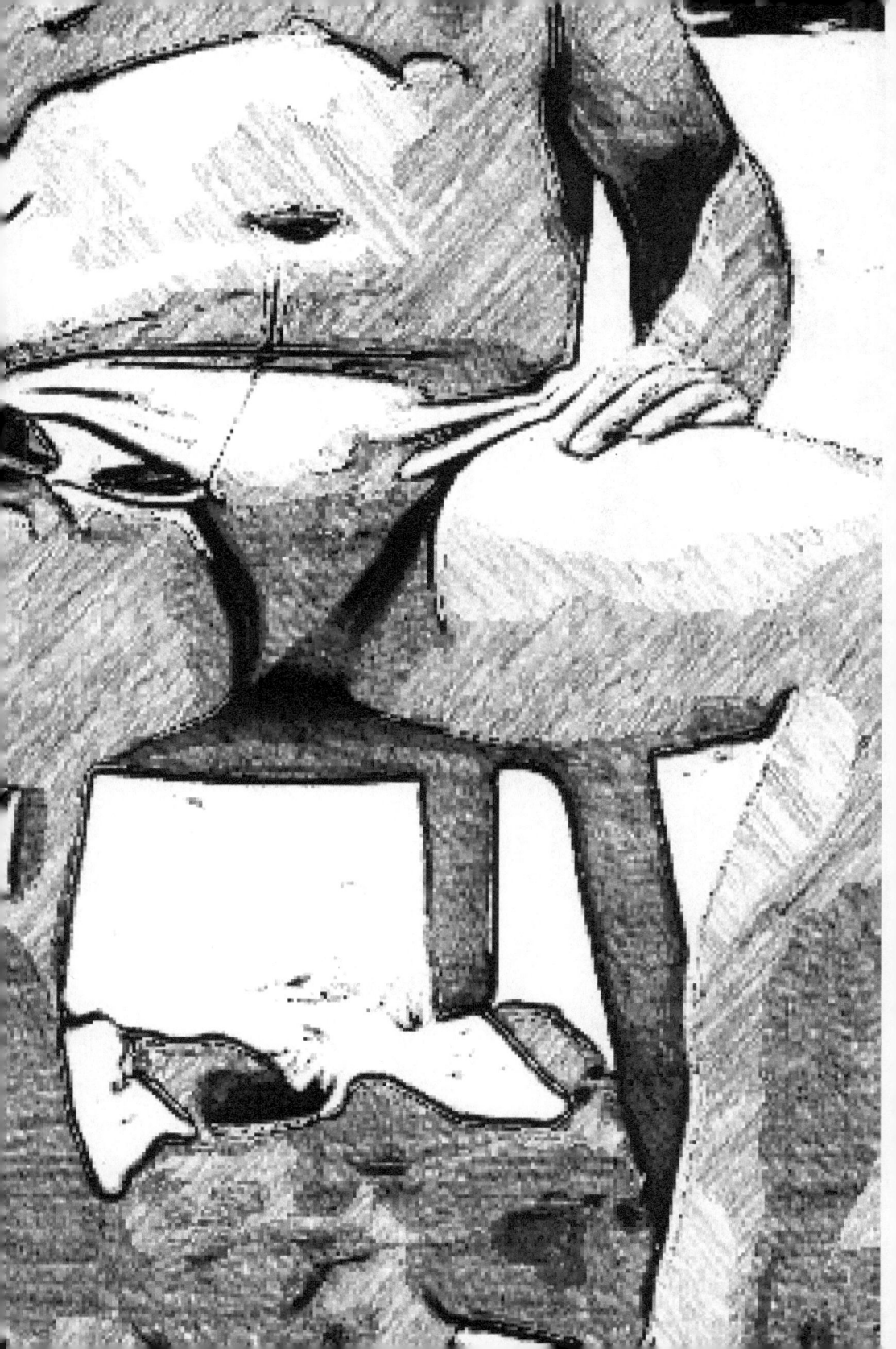

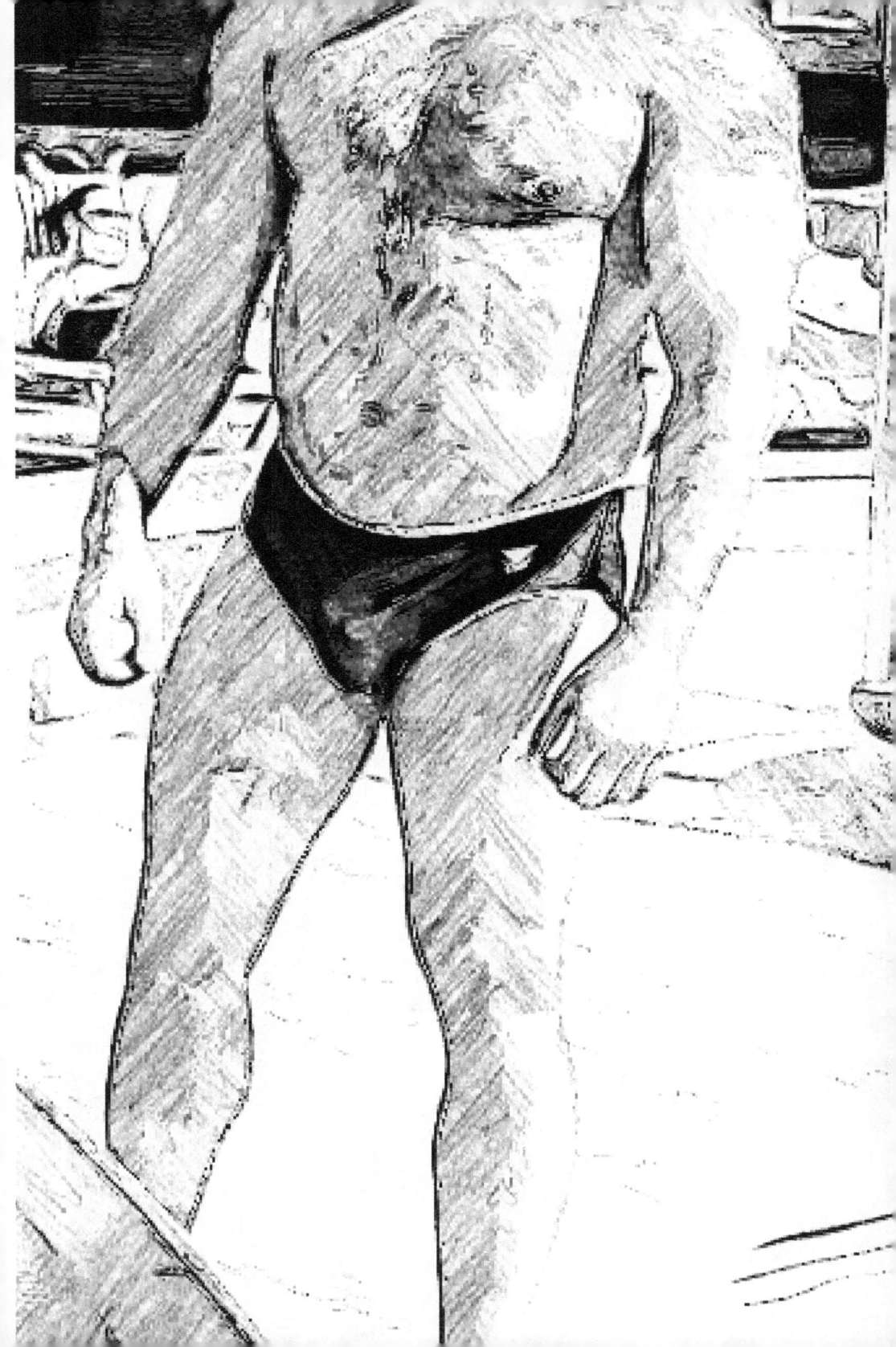

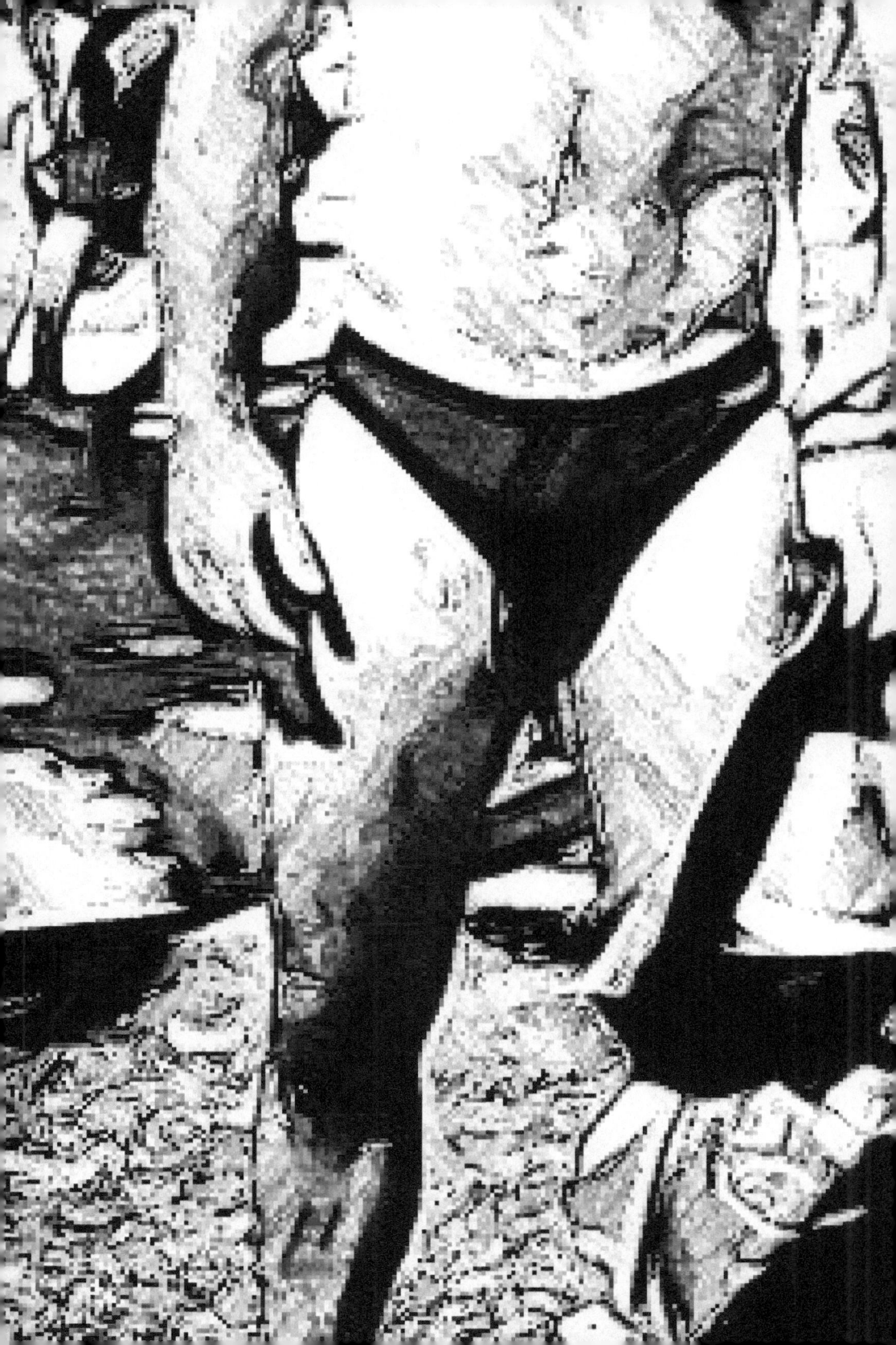

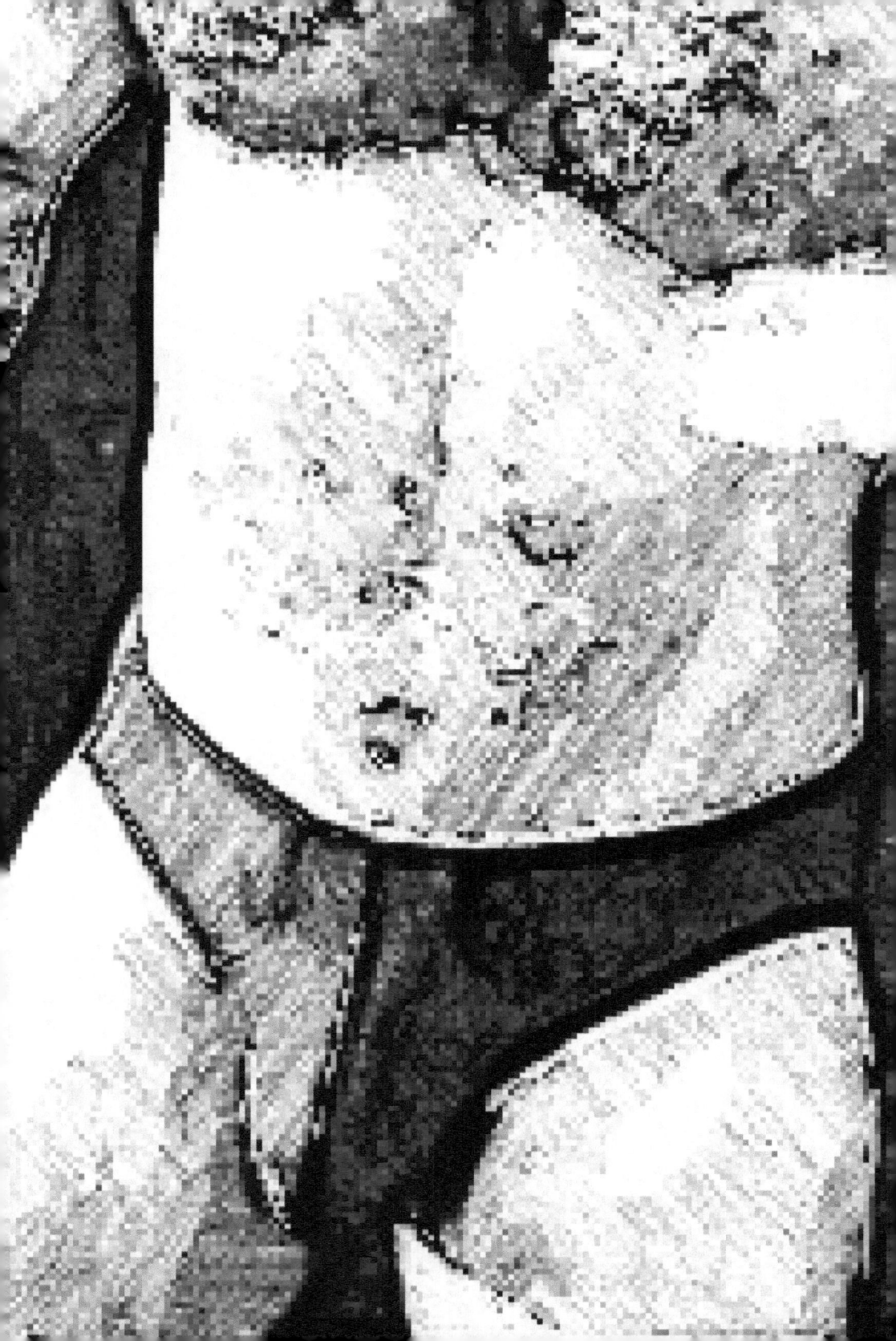

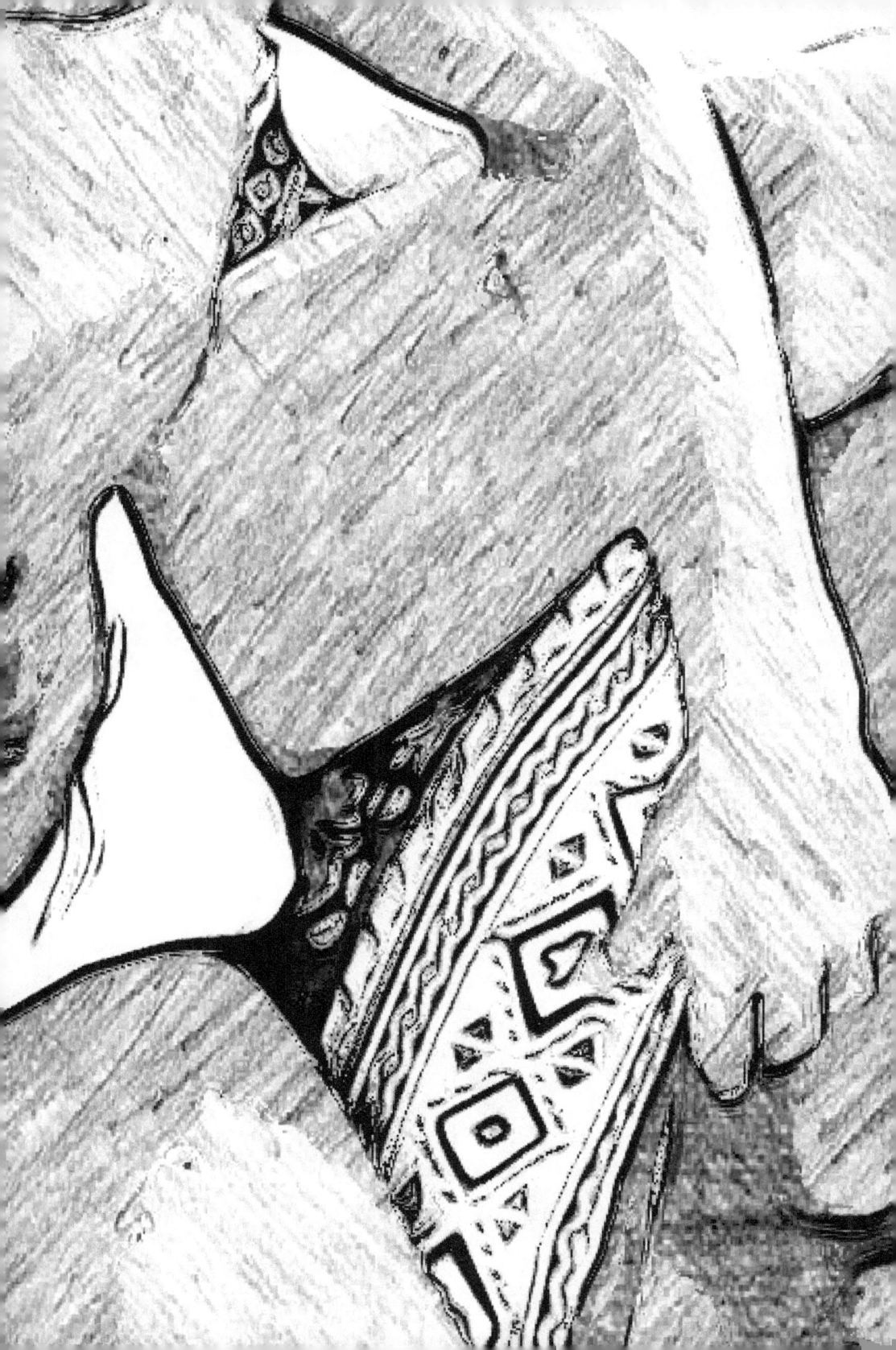

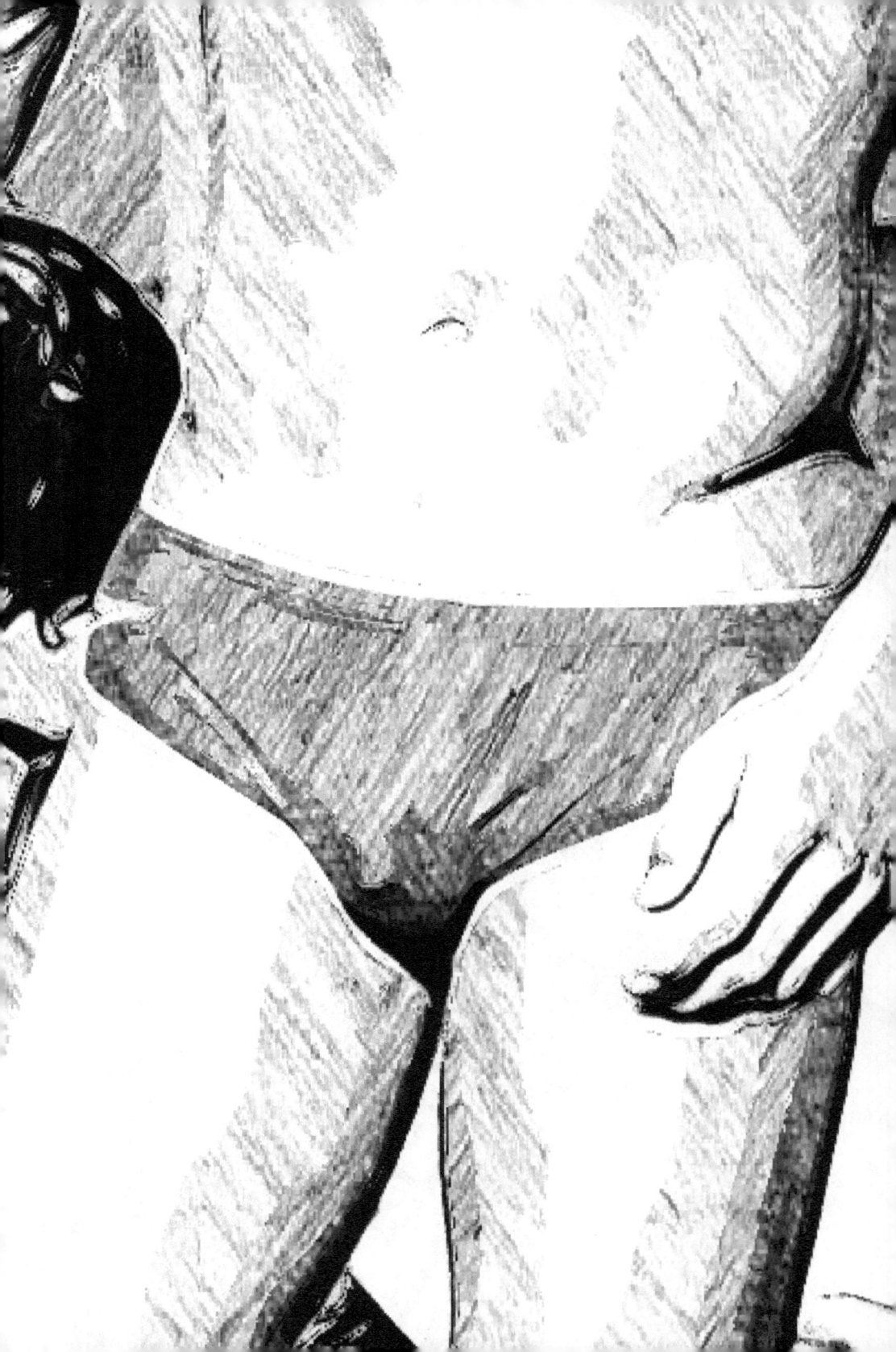

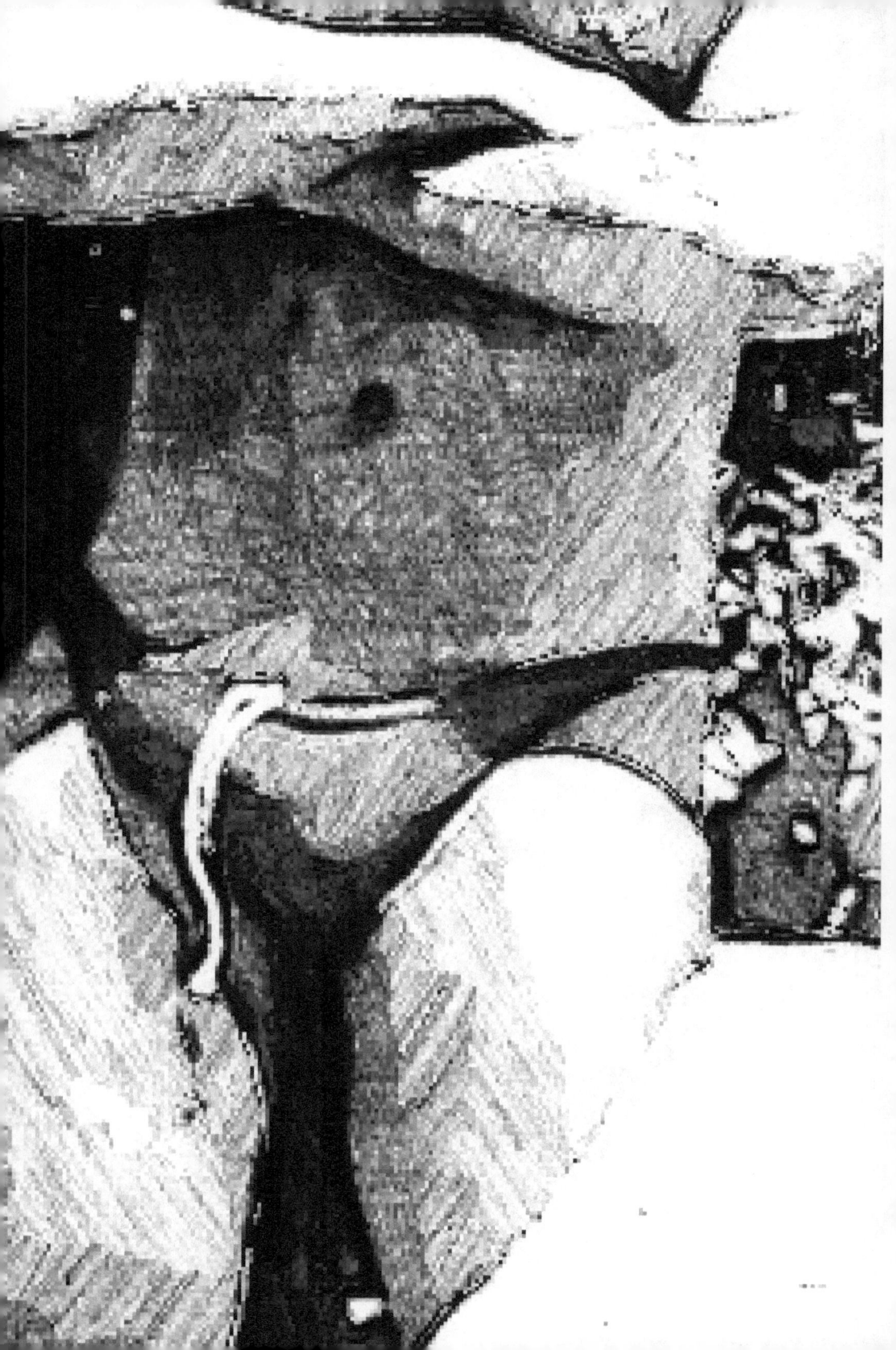

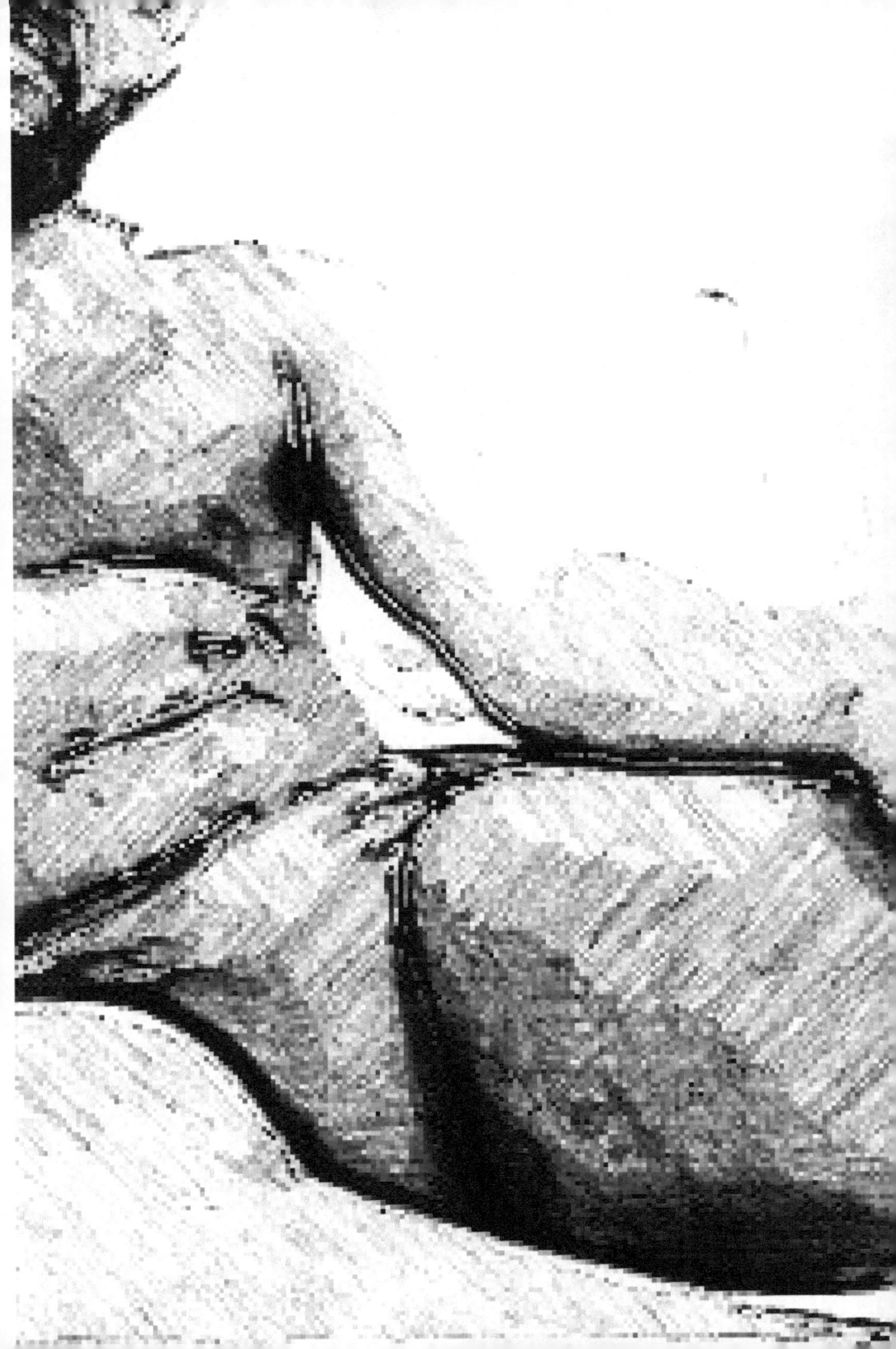

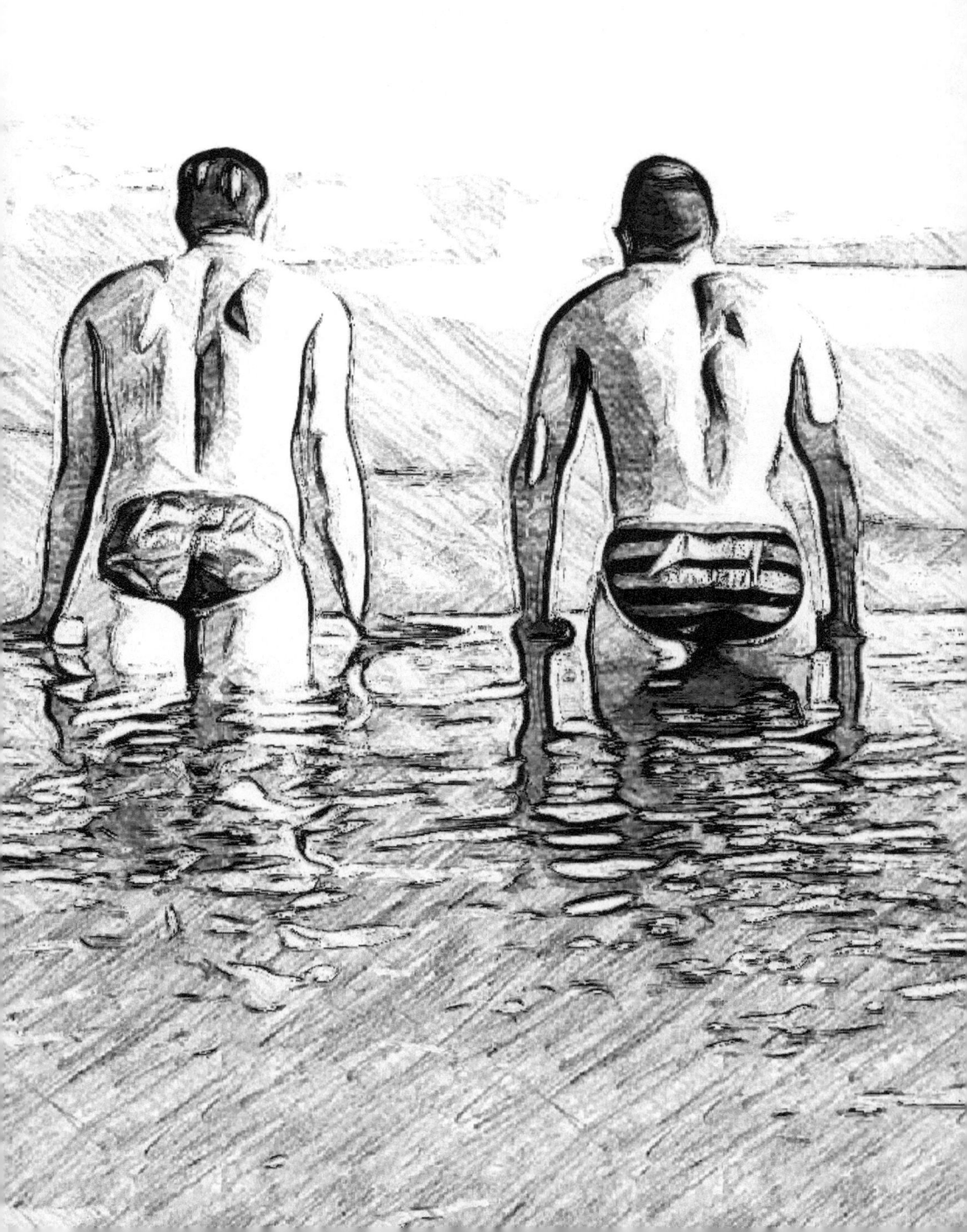

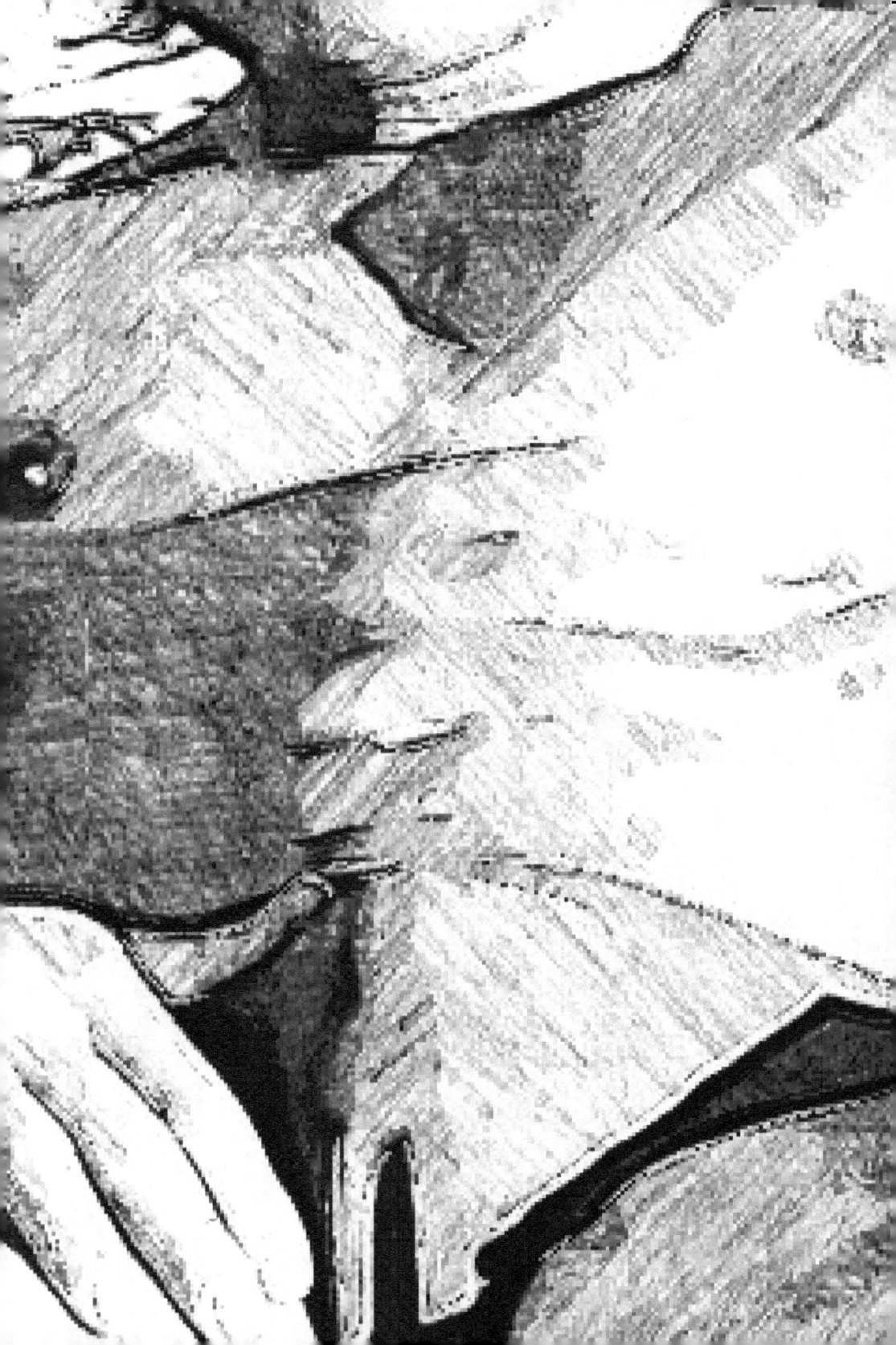

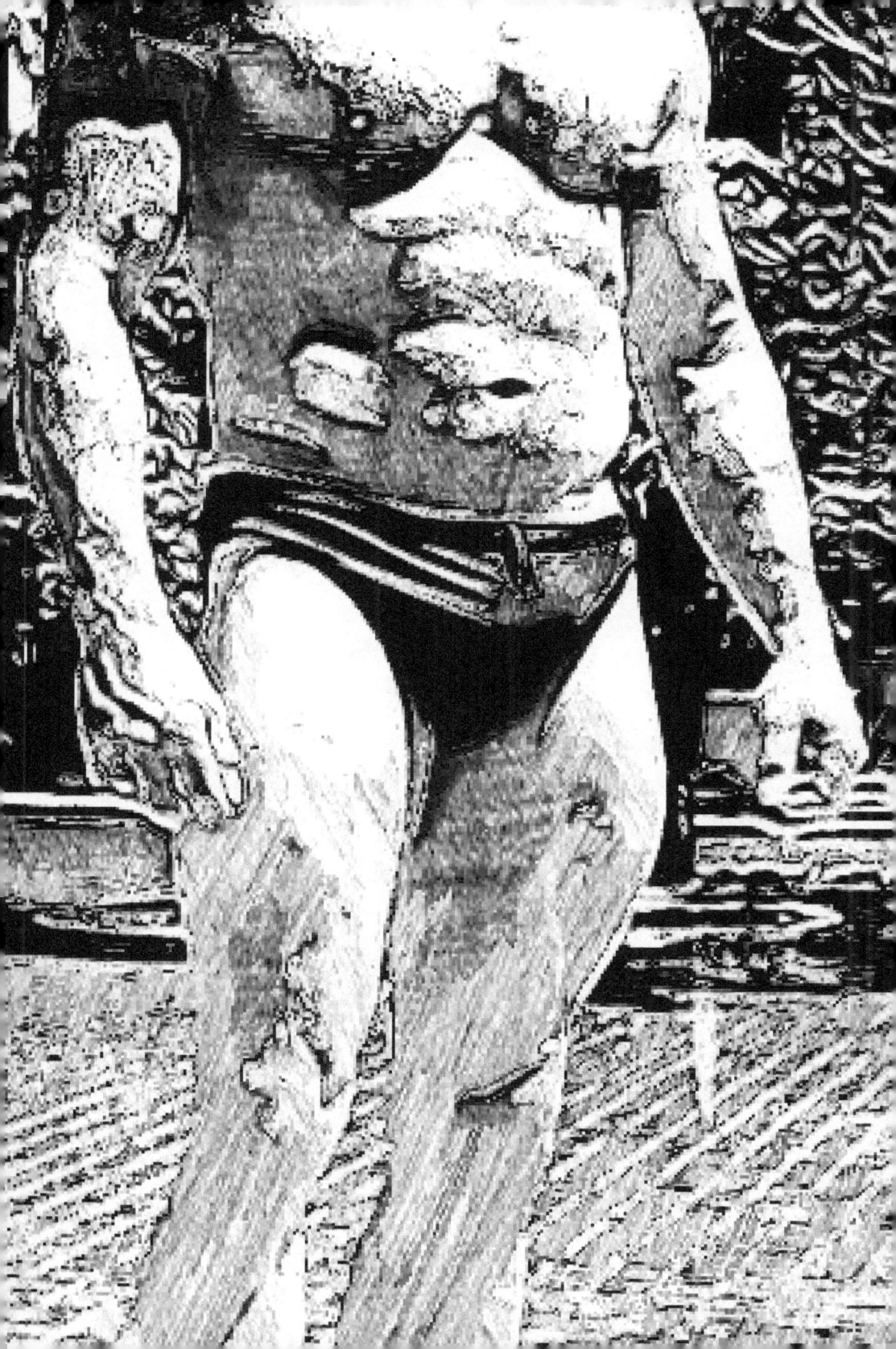

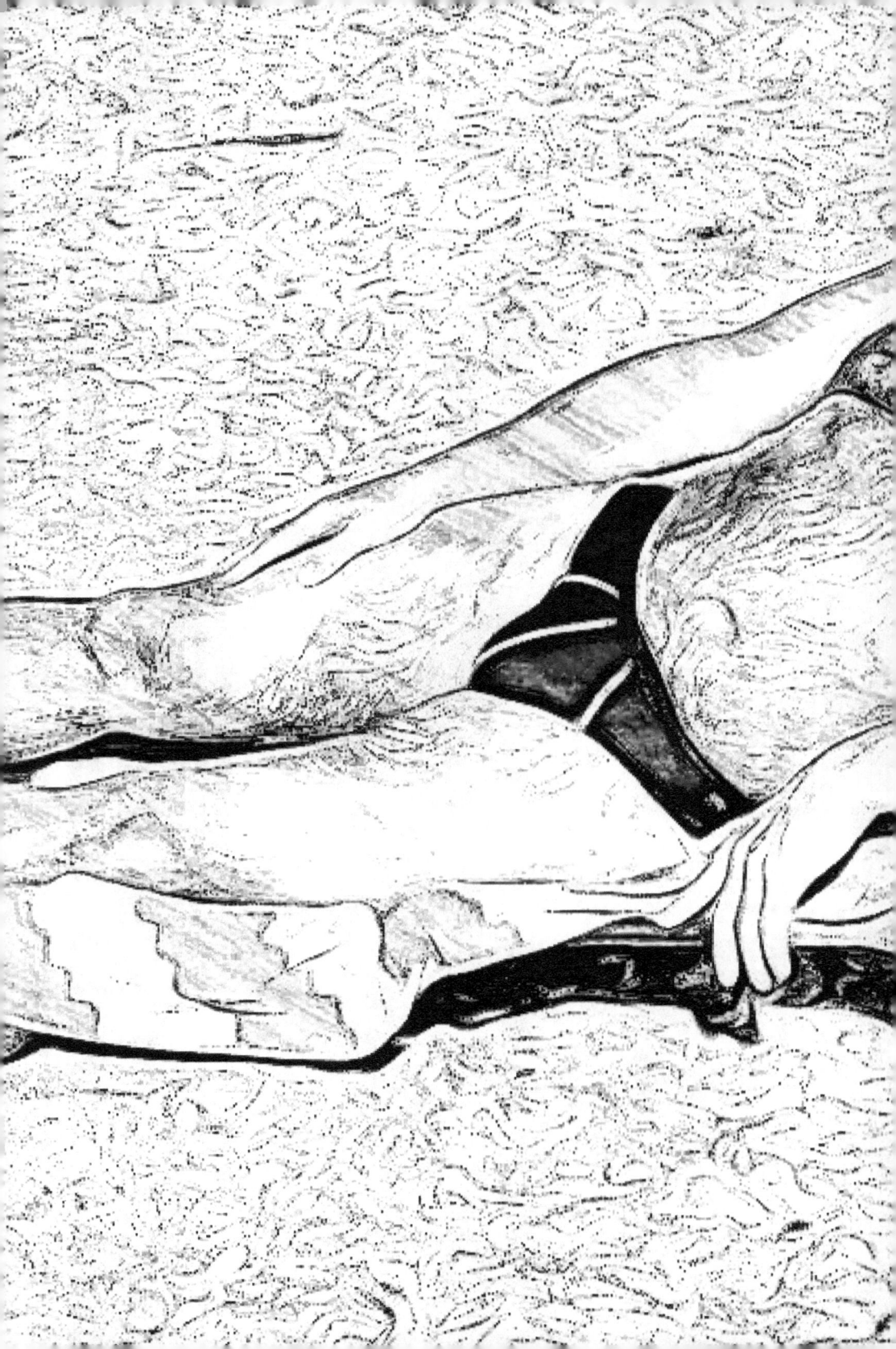

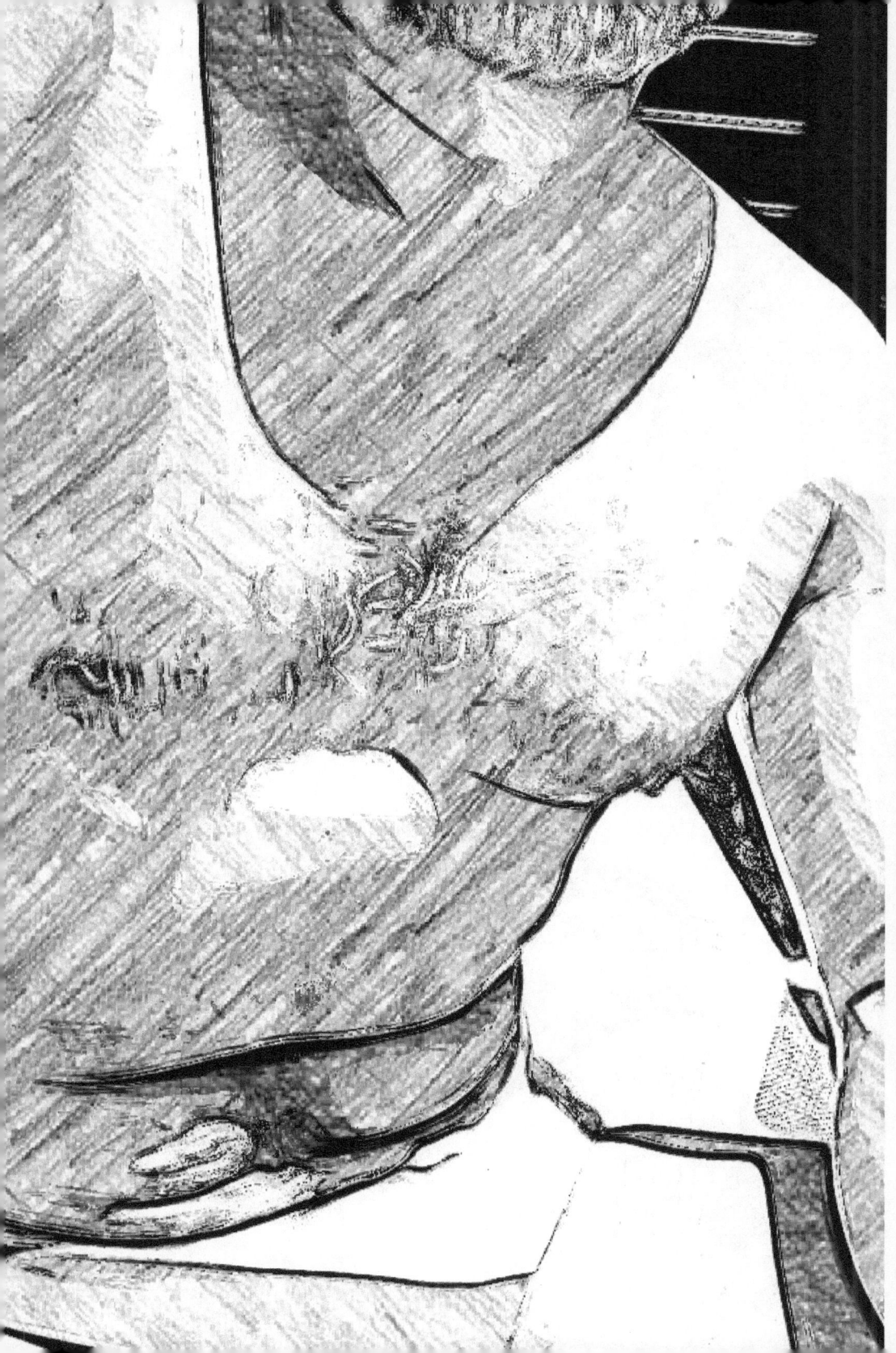

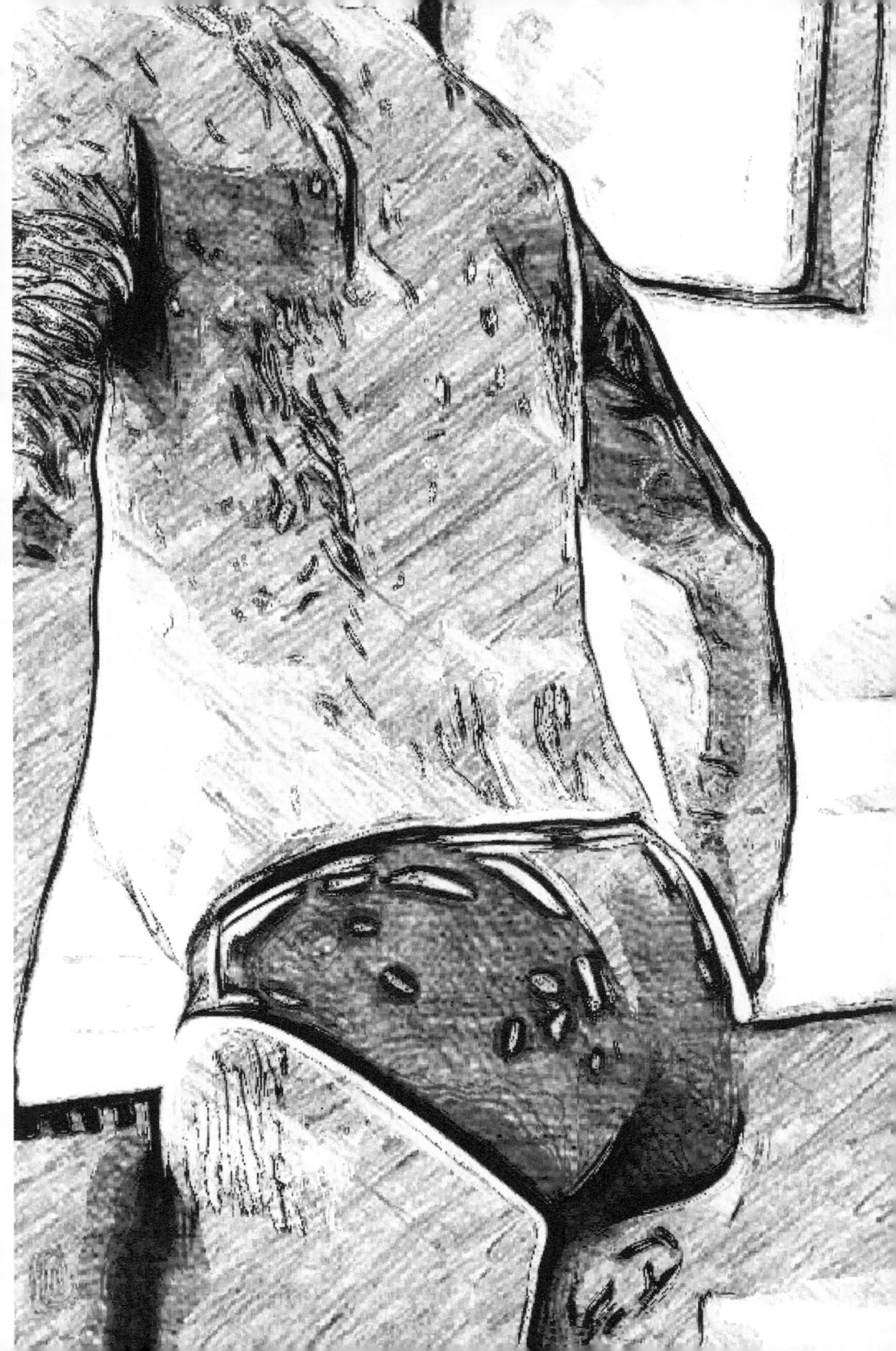

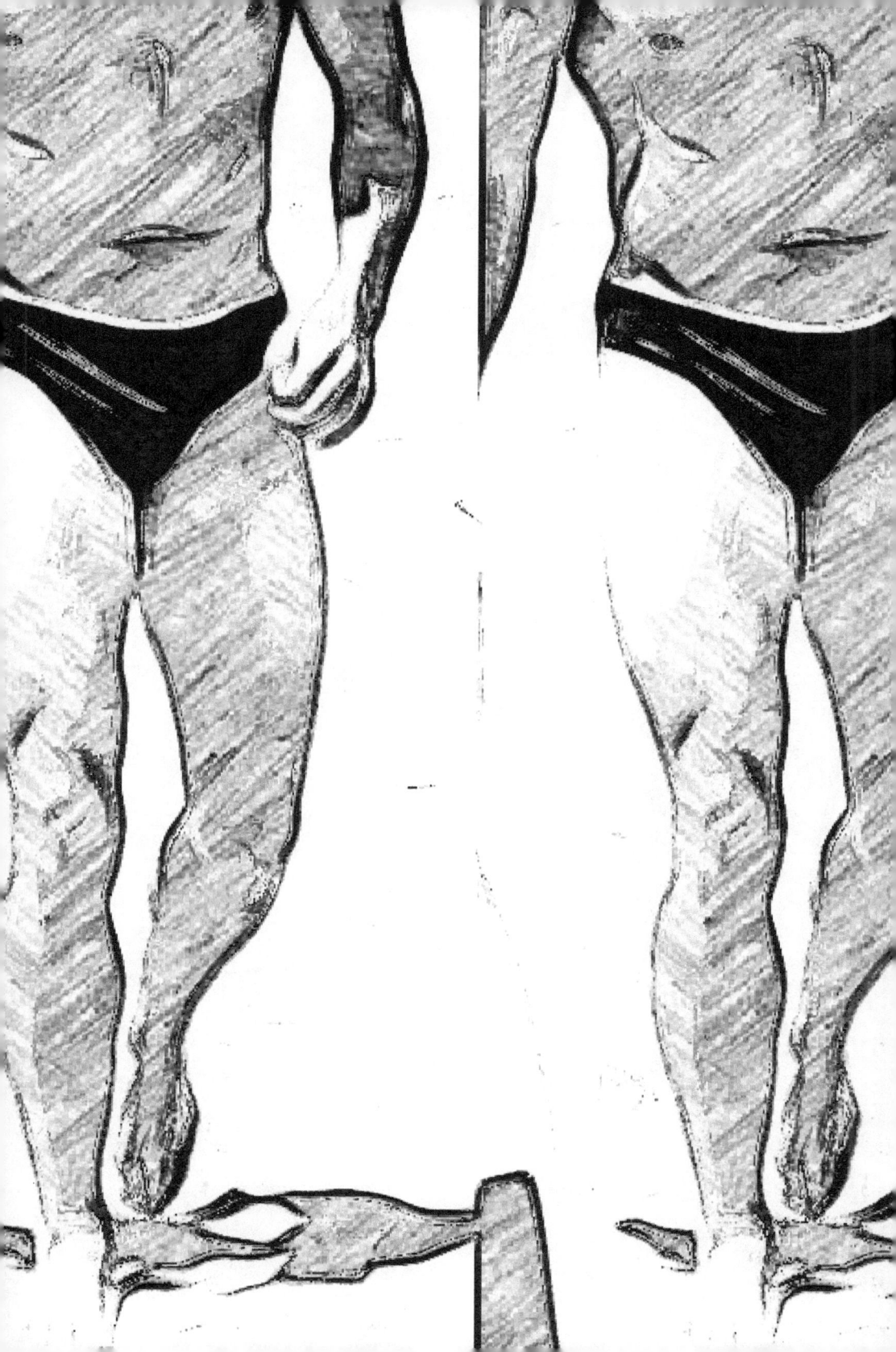

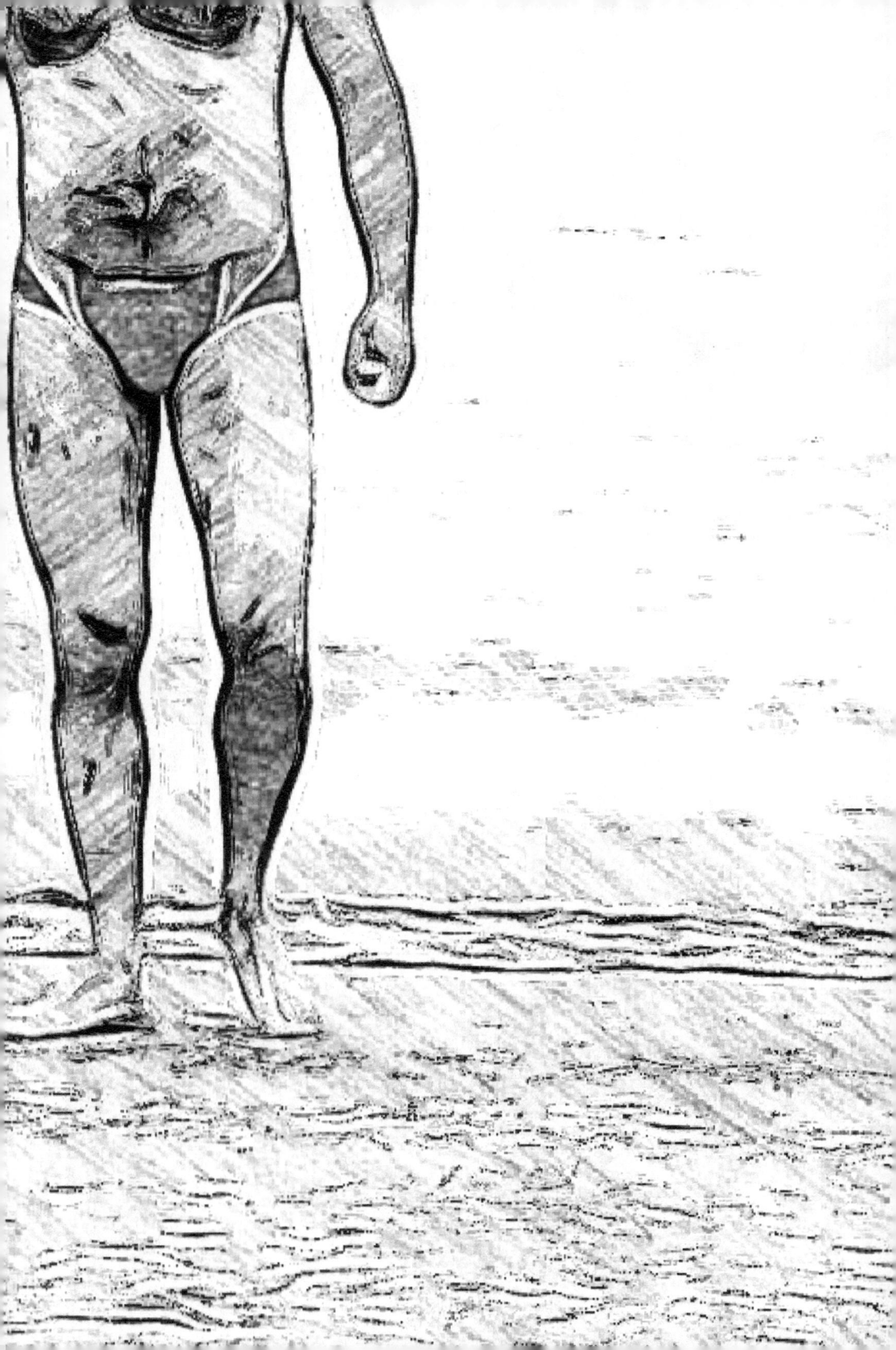

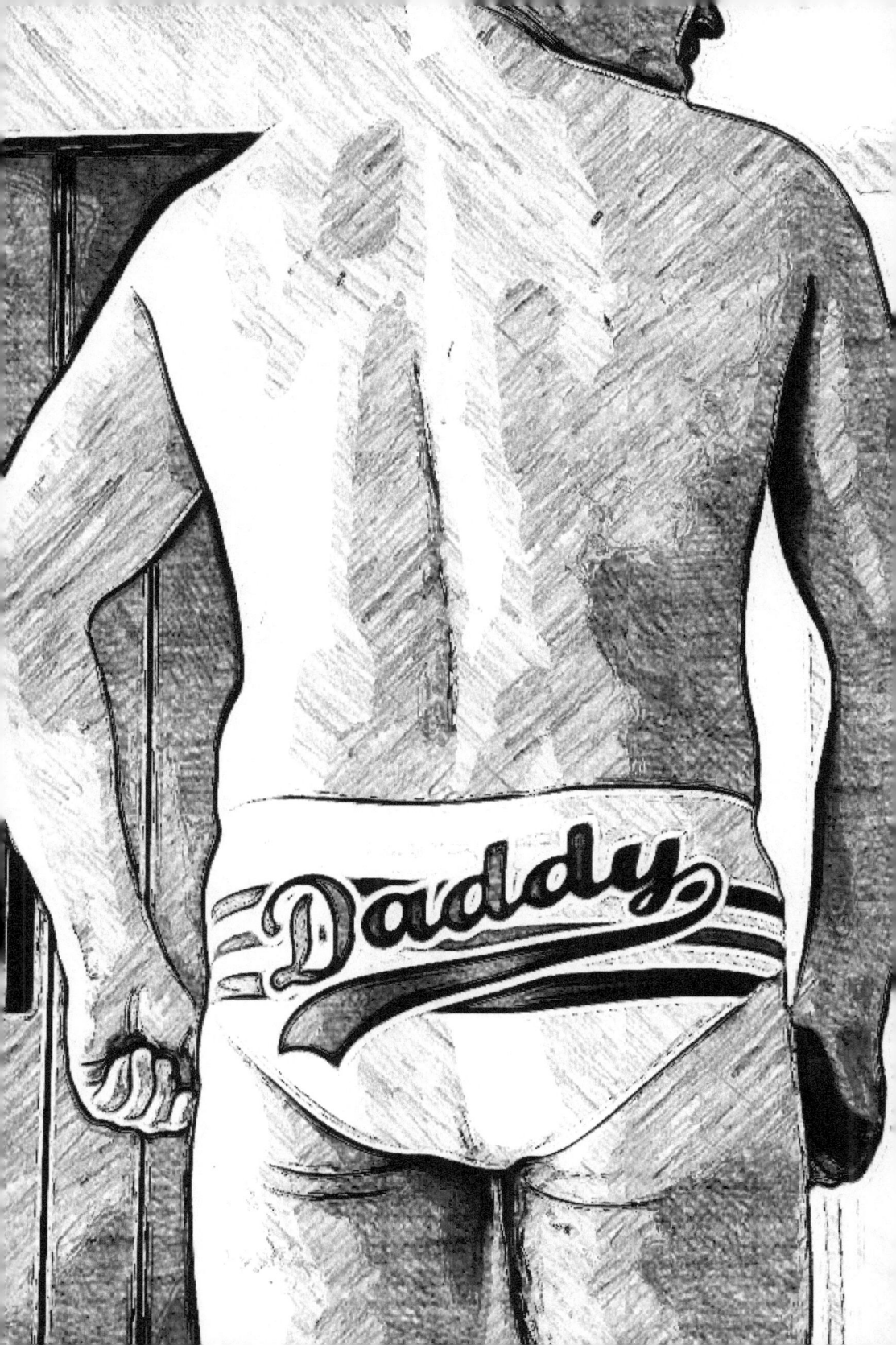

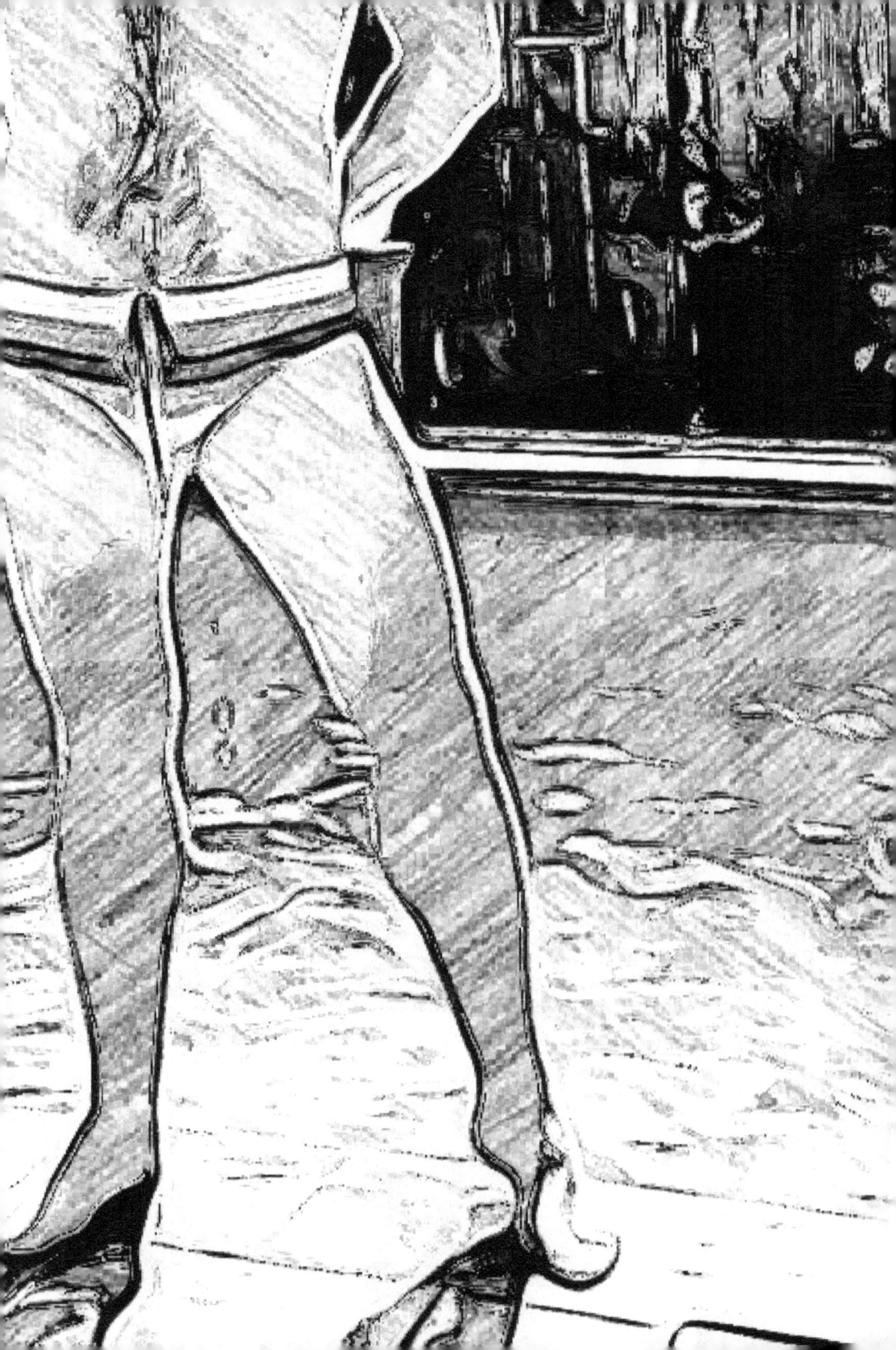

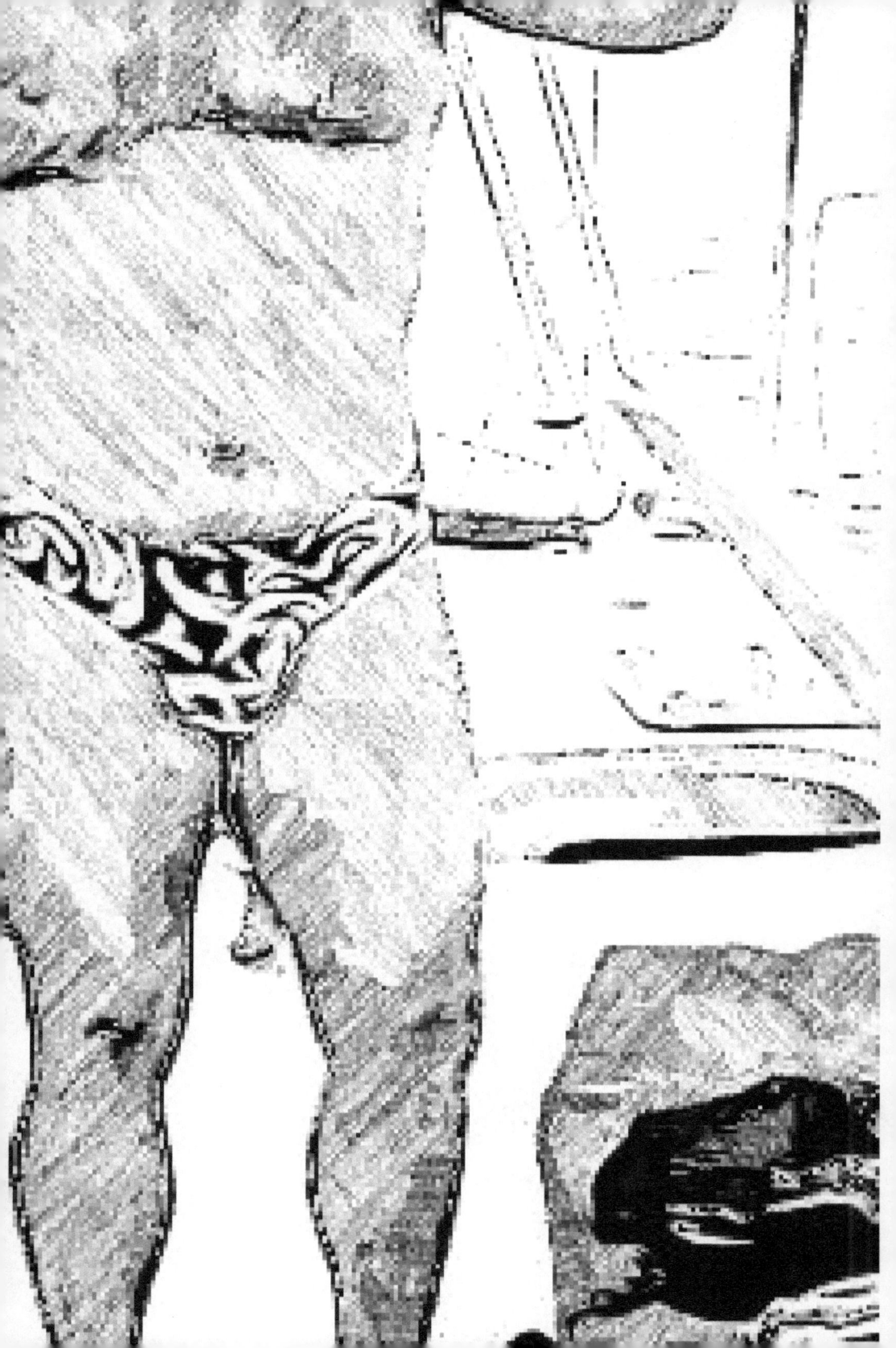

www.ingramcontent.com/pod-product-compliance
Lightning Source LLC
Chambersburg PA
CBHW021020180526
45163CB00005B/2034